The tragedy of Valentinian. Written by Mr. Francis Beaumont, and Mr. John Fletcher.

John Fletcher

PRINT EDITIONS

Eighteenth Century
Collections Online
Print Editions

Gale ECCO Print Editions

Relive history with *Eighteenth Century Collections Online*, now available in print for the independent historian and collector. This series includes the most significant English-language and foreign-language works printed in Great Britain during the eighteenth century, and is organized in seven different subject areas including literature and language; medicine, science, and technology; and religion and philosophy. The collection also includes thousands of important works from the Americas.

The eighteenth century has been called "The Age of Enlightenment." It was a period of rapid advance in print culture and publishing, in world exploration, and in the rapid growth of science and technology – all of which had a profound impact on the political and cultural landscape. At the end of the century the American Revolution, French Revolution and Industrial Revolution, perhaps three of the most significant events in modern history, set in motion developments that eventually dominated world political, economic, and social life.

In a groundbreaking effort, Gale initiated a revolution of its own: digitization of epic proportions to preserve these invaluable works in the largest online archive of its kind. Contributions from major world libraries constitute over 175,000 original printed works. Scanned images of the actual pages, rather than transcriptions, recreate the works *as they first appeared.*

Now for the first time, these high-quality digital scans of original works are available via print-on-demand, making them readily accessible to libraries, students, independent scholars, and readers of all ages.

For our initial release we have created seven robust collections to form one the world's most comprehensive catalogs of 18th century works.

Initial Gale ECCO Print Editions collections include:

History and Geography
Rich in titles on English life and social history, this collection spans the world as it was known to eighteenth-century historians and explorers. Titles include a wealth of travel accounts and diaries, histories of nations from throughout the world, and maps and charts of a world that was still being discovered. Students of the War of American Independence will find fascinating accounts from the British side of conflict.

Social Science

Delve into what it was like to live during the eighteenth century by reading the first-hand accounts of everyday people, including city dwellers and farmers, businessmen and bankers, artisans and merchants, artists and their patrons, politicians and their constituents. Original texts make the American, French, and Industrial revolutions vividly contemporary.

Medicine, Science and Technology

Medical theory and practice of the 1700s developed rapidly, as is evidenced by the extensive collection, which includes descriptions of diseases, their conditions, and treatments. Books on science and technology, agriculture, military technology, natural philosophy, even cookbooks, are all contained here.

Literature and Language

Western literary study flows out of eighteenth-century works by Alexander Pope, Daniel Defoe, Henry Fielding, Frances Burney, Denis Diderot, Johann Gottfried Herder, Johann Wolfgang von Goethe, and others. Experience the birth of the modern novel, or compare the development of language using dictionaries and grammar discourses.

Religion and Philosophy

The Age of Enlightenment profoundly enriched religious and philosophical understanding and continues to influence present-day thinking. Works collected here include masterpieces by David Hume, Immanuel Kant, and Jean-Jacques Rousseau, as well as religious sermons and moral debates on the issues of the day, such as the slave trade. The Age of Reason saw conflict between Protestantism and Catholicism transformed into one between faith and logic -- a debate that continues in the twenty-first century.

Law and Reference

This collection reveals the history of English common law and Empire law in a vastly changing world of British expansion. Dominating the legal field is the *Commentaries of the Law of England* by Sir William Blackstone, which first appeared in 1765. Reference works such as almanacs and catalogues continue to educate us by revealing the day-to-day workings of society.

Fine Arts

The eighteenth-century fascination with Greek and Roman antiquity followed the systematic excavation of the ruins at Pompeii and Herculaneum in southern Italy; and after 1750 a neoclassical style dominated all artistic fields. The titles here trace developments in mostly English-language works on painting, sculpture, architecture, music, theater, and other disciplines. Instructional works on musical instruments, catalogs of art objects, comic operas, and more are also included.

The BiblioLife Network

This project was made possible in part by the BiblioLife Network (BLN), a project aimed at addressing some of the huge challenges facing book preservationists around the world. The BLN includes libraries, library networks, archives, subject matter experts, online communities and library service providers. We believe every book ever published should be available as a high-quality print reproduction; printed on-demand anywhere in the world. This insures the ongoing accessibility of the content and helps generate sustainable revenue for the libraries and organizations that work to preserve these important materials.

The following book is in the "public domain" and represents an authentic reproduction of the text as printed by the original publisher. While we have attempted to accurately maintain the integrity of the original work, there are sometimes problems with the original work or the micro-film from which the books were digitized. This can result in minor errors in reproduction. Possible imperfections include missing and blurred pages, poor pictures, markings and other reproduction issues beyond our control. Because this work is culturally important, we have made it available as part of our commitment to protecting, preserving, and promoting the world's literature.

GUIDE TO FOLD-OUTS MAPS and OVERSIZED IMAGES

The book you are reading was digitized from microfilm captured over the past thirty to forty years. Years after the creation of the original microfilm, the book was converted to digital files and made available in an online database.

In an online database, page images do not need to conform to the size restrictions found in a printed book. When converting these images back into a printed bound book, the page sizes are standardized in ways that maintain the detail of the original. For large images, such as fold-out maps, the original page image is split into two or more pages

Guidelines used to determine how to split the page image follows:

• Some images are split vertically; large images require vertical and horizontal splits.
• For horizontal splits, the content is split left to right.
• For vertical splits, the content is split from top to bottom.
• For both vertical and horizontal splits, the image is processed from top left to bottom right.

THE

TRAGEDY

OF

VALENTINIAN.

Written by

Mr. *FRANCIS BEAUMONT,*

AND

Mr. *JOHN FLETCHER.*

LONDON,

Printed for *J. T.* And Sold by *J. Brown* at the *Black Swan* without *Temple-Bar.* 1717.

Dramatis Personæ.

MEN.

Valentinian, *Emperor of* Rome.
Æcius, *the Emperor's Loyal General.*
Balbus,
Proculus, } *Four Noble Panders, and Flatterers to the*
Chilax, } *Emperor.*
Licinius,
Maximus, *a great Soldier, Husband to* Lucina.
Lycias, *an Eunuch.*
Pontius, *an honest Cashier'd Centurion.*
Phidias, } *two bold and faithful Eunuchs, Servants*
Aretus, } *to* Æcius.
Afranius, *an eminent Captain.*
Paulus, *a Poet.*
Licippus, *a Courtier.*

WOMEN.

Eudoxia, *Empress, Wife to* Valentinian.
Lucina, *the chaste abused Wife of* Maximus.
Claudia, } Lucina's *Waiting-women.*
Marcellina,
Ardelia } *two of the Emperor's Bawds.*
Phorba,
Three Senators, Physicians, Gentlemen and Soldiers.

SCENE ROME.

THE

THE
TRAGEDY
OF
VALENTINIAN.

ACT I. SCENE I.

Enter Balbus, Proculus, Chilax *and* Licinius.

Balb. I Never faw the like, fhe's no more ftir'd,
No more another Woman, no more alter'd,
With any hopes or promifes laid to her,
Let 'em be ne'er fo weighty, ne'er fo winning,
Than I am with the motion of my own Legs.
  Pro. Chilax,
You are a Stranger yet in thefe defigns,
At leaft in *Rome;* tell me, and tell me truth,
Did you e'er know in all your courfe of practice,
In all the ways of Woman you have run through,
(For I prefume you have been brought up, *Chilax,*
As we, to fetch and carry.)
  Chi. True, I have fo.
  Pro. Did you, I fay again, in all this progrefs,
Ever difcover fuch a piece of Beauty,
Ever fo rare a Creature, and no doubt,
One that muft know her worth too, and affect it,
Ay and be flatter'd, elfe 'tis none; and honeft ?
Honeft againft the Tide of all Temptations,
Honeft to one Man, to her Husband only,
And yet not eighteen, not of Age to know
Why fhe is honeft?

A 2

Chi.

Chi. I confeſs it freely,
I never ſaw her fellow, nor e'er ſhall:
For all our *Grœcian* Dames, all I have try'd,
(And ſure I have try'd a hundred, if I ſay two
I ſpeak within my Compaſs) all theſe Beauties,
And all the conſtancy of all theſe Faces,
Maids, Widows, Wives, of what degree or calling,
So they be *Greeks*, and fat, for there's my cunning,
I would undertake and not ſweat for't, *Proculus*,
Were they to try again, ſay twice as many,
Under a thouſand Pound, to lay 'em Bed-rid;
But this Wench ſtaggers me.

Lyc. Do you ſee theſe Jewels?
You would think theſe pretty baits; now I'll aſſure ye
Here's half the Wealth of *Aſia*.

Bal. Theſe are nothing
To the full Honours I propounded to her;
I bid her think, and be, and preſently
Whatever her Ambition, what the Council
Of others would add to her, what her Dreams
Could more enlarge, what any Precedent
Of any Woman riſing up to Glory,
And ſtanding certain there, and in the higheſt,
Could give her more, nay, to be Empreſs.

Pro. And cold at all theſe Offers?

Bal. Cold as Chriſtal,
Never to be thraw'd again.

Chi I try'd her further,
And ſo far, that I think ſhe is no Woman,
At leaſt as Women go now.

Lyc. Why what did you?

Chi. I offer'd that, that had ſhe been but Miſtreſs
Of as much Spleen as Doves have, I had reach'd her;
A ſafe Revenge of all that ever hate her,
The crying down for ever of all Beauties
That may be thought come near her.

Pro. That was pretty.

Chi. I never knew that way fail; yet I'll tell you
I offer'd her a Gift beyond all your,
That, that had made a Saint ſtirt, well conſider'd;
The Law to be her Creature, ſhe to make it,
Her Mouth to give it, every Creature living
From her Aſpect to draw their good or evil,
Fix'd in 'em ſpight of Fortune; a new Nature
She ſhould be call'd, and Mother of all Ages,
Time ſhould be hers, and what ſhe did lame Virtue

Should

Should bless to all Posterities: Her Air,
Should give us Life, her Earth and Water feed us;
And last, to none but to the Emperor,
(And then but when she pleas'd to have it so,)
She should be held for mortal.

　　Lyc. And she heard you?
　　Chi. Yes, as a sick Man hears a noise, or he
That stands condemn'd his Judgment; let me perish,
But if there can be Virtue, if that Name
Be any thing but Name and empty Title,
If it be so as Fools have been pleas'd to feign it,
A Power that can preserve us after Ashes,
And make the Names of Men out-reckon Ages;
This Woman has a God of Virtue in her.

　　Bal. I would the Emperor were that God.
　　Chi. She has in her
All the contempt of Glory and vain seeming
Of all the *Stoicks*, all the Truth of Christians,
And all their Constancy. Modesty was made
When she was first intended: When she blushes
It is the holiest thing to look upon;
The purest Temple of her Sect, that ever
Made Nature a blest Founder.

　　Pro. Is there no way
To take this *Phenix*?
　　Lyc. None but in her Ashes.
　　Chi. If she were fat, or any way inclining
To Ease or Pleasure, or affected Glory,
Proud to be seen and worship'd, 'twere a venture;
But on my Soul she's chaster than cold Camphire.

　　Bal. I think so too; for all the ways of Woman,
Like a full Sail, she bears against: I ask'd her
After my many Offers, walking with her,
And her as many down-denials, how
If the Emperor, grown mad with Love, should force her;
She pointed to a *Lucrece*, that hung by,
And with an angry look, that from her Eyes
Shot Vestal fire against me, she departed.

　　Pro. This is the first Wench I was ever pos'd in,
Yet I have brought young loving things together
This two and thirty Year.
　　Chi. I find by this Wench
The Calling of a Bawd to be a strange,
A wise, and subtile Calling; and for none
But staid, discreet, and understanding People:
And, as the Tutor to great *Alexander*

　　　　　　　　　　　　　　　　Would

Would fay, a young Man fhould not dare to read
His Moral Books, till after five and twenty;
So muft that he or fhe, that will be bawdy,
(I mean difcreetly bawdy, and be trufted)
If they will rife, and gain Experience,
Well ftept in Years, and Difcipline, begin it,
I take it 'tis no Boys play.

 Bal. Well, what's thought of ?
 Pho. The Emperor muft know it.
 Lyc. If the Women fhould chance to fail too.
 Chi. As 'tis ten to one.
 Pro. Why what remains, but new Nets for the purchafe ?
 Chi. Let's go confider then ; and if all fail,
This is the firft quick Eel, that fav'd her Tail.   [*Exe.*

SCENE II.

Enter Lucina, Ardelia, *and* Phorba.

 Ard. You ftill infift upon that Idol, Honour,
Can it renew your Youth, can it add Wealth.
That takes off Wrinkles; can it draw Mens Eyes
To gaze upon you in your Age? Can Honour,
That truly is a Saint to none but Soldiers,
And look'd into, bears no Reward but Danger,
Leave you the moft refpected Perfon living?
Or can the common kiffes of a Husband,
(Which to a fprightly Lady is a labour)
Make ye almoft Immortal? Ye are cozen'd,
The Honour of a Woman is her Praifes;
The way to get thefe, to be feen, and fought to,
And not to bury fuch a happy Sweetnefs
Under a fmoaky Roof.

 Luc. I'll hear no more.
 Phor. That White, and Red, and all that bliffed Beauty,
Kept from the Eyes, that make it fo, is nothing:
Then you are rarely fair, when Men proclaim it;
The *Phenix*, were fhe never feen, were doubted.
That moft unvalued Horn the Unicorn
Bears to oppofe the Huntfman, were it nothing
But Tale, and meer Tradition, would help no Man ;
But when the Virtue's known, the Honour's doubled:
Virtue is either lame, or not at all,
And Love a Sacrilege, and not a Saint,
When it bars up the way to Mens Petitions.

 Ard. Nay, ye fhall love your Husband too; we come not
To make a Monfter of ye.

 Luc. Are ye Women?

                Ard.

Ard. You'll find us, so, and Women you shall thank too,
If you have Grace to make your use.

Luc. Fye on ye.

Phor. Alas, poor bashful Lady! By my Soul,
Had ye no other Virtue but your Blushes,
And I a Man, I should run mad for those:
How daintily they set her off, how sweetly!

Ard. Come Goddess, come, you move too near the Earth,
I must not be, a better Orb stays for you:
Here; be a Maid, and take 'em.

Luc. Pray leave me.

Phor. That were a sin, sweet Lady, and a way
To make us guilty of your Melancholy;
You must not be alone; in Conversation
Doubts are resolv'd, and what sticks near the Conscience
Made easie, and allowable

Luc. Ye are Devils.

Ard. That you may one day bless for your damnation.

Luc. I charge ye in the name of Chastity,
Tempt me no more; how ugly ye seem to me?
There is no wonder Men defame our Sex,
And lay the Vices of all Ages on us,
When such as you shall bear the Names of Women:
If ye had Eyes to see your selves, or Sense
Above the base Rewards ye play the Bawds for;
If ever in your lives ye heard of Goodness,
Though many Regions off, as Men hear Thunder;
If ever ye had Mothers, and they Souls;
If ever Fathers, and not such as you are;
If ever any thing were constant in you,
Beside your Sins, or coming but your Courses,
If ever any of your Ancestors
Dy'd worth a noble deed, that would be cherish'd,
Soul-frighted with this black Infection,
You would run from one another, to Repentance,
And from your guilty Eyes drop out those Sins,
That made ye blind, and Beasts.

Phor. Ye speak well, Lady;
A sign of fruitful Education,
If your religious Zeal had Wisdom with it.

Ard. This Lady was ordain'd to bless the Empire,
And we may all give thanks for't.

Phor. I believe ye.

Ard. If any thing redeem the Emperor
From his wild flying Courses, this is she;
She can instruct him, if ye mark; she is wise too.

Phor.

Phor. Exceeding wife, which is a wonder in her,
And so religious, that I well believe,
Though she would sin she cannot.

Ard. And besides,
She has the Empire's Cause in hand, not Love's;
There lies the main Confideration,
For which she is chiefly born.

Phor. She finds that point
Stronger than we can tell her, and believe it
I look by her means for a Reformation,
And such a one, and such a rare way carried,
That all the World shall wonder at.

Ard. 'Tis true;
I never thought the Emperor had Wisdom,
Pity, or fair Affection to his Country,
'Till he profest this Love: Gods give 'em Children,
Such as her Virtues merit, and his Zeal.
I look to see a *Numa* from this Lady,
Or greater than *Octavius*.

Phor. Do you mark too,
Which is a noble Virtue; how she blushes,
And what a flowing Modesty runs through her,
When we but name the Emperor?

Ard. But mark it,
Yes, and admire it too; for she confiders,
Though she be fair as Heav'n, and virtuous
As holy Truth, yet to the Emperor
She is a kind of nothing but her Service,
Which she is bound to offer, and she'll do it;
And when her Country's Cause commands Affection,
She knows Obedience is the Key of Virtues,
Then fly the Blushes out like *Cupid's* Arrows:
And though the tye of Marriage to her Lord
Would fain cry, Stay *Lucina*; yet the Cause,
And general Wisdom of the Prince's Love,
Makes her find furer Ends, and happier;
And if the first were chaste, this is twice doubled.

Phor. Her Tartness unto us too.

Ard. That's a wife one.

Phor. I rarely like, it shews a rifing Wisdom,
That chides all common Fools as dare enquire
What Princes would have private.

Ard. What a Lady
Shall we be blest to serve?

Luc. Go, get ye from me.
Ye are your Purses Agents, not the Prince's:

Is this the virtuous Lore ye train'd me out to?
Am I a Woman fit to imp your Vices?
But that I had a Mother, and a Woman,
Whose ever-living Fame turns all it touches,
Into the good it self is, I should now
Even doubt my self, I have been search'd so near
The very soul of Honour: Why should you two,
That happily have been as chaſt as I am,
Fairer I think by much, for yet your Faces,
Like ancient well-built Piles, shew worthy Ruins,
After that Angel-Age, turn mortal Devils?
For shame, for Woman-hood, for what ye have been,
For rotten Cedars have born goodly Branches;
If ye have hope of any Heav'n, but Court,
Which like a Dream, you'll find hereafter vanish,
Or at the best, but subject to Repentance,
Study no more to be ill spoken of;
Let Women live themselves; if they muſt fall,
Their own Deſtruction find 'em, not your Feavers.

   Ard. Madam, ye are so excellent in all,
And I muſt tell it you with admiration,
So true a Joy ye have, so sweat a Fear,
And when ye come to Anger, 'tis so noble,
That for mine own Part, I could ſtill offend,
To hear you angry; Women that want that,
And your way guided (elſe I count it nothing)
Are either Fools or Cowards.

   Phor. She were a Miſtreſs for no private Greatneſs,
Could she not frown a raviſh'd Kiſs from Anger:
And such an Anger as this Lady learns us,
Stuck with such pleaſing Dangers, Gods, I aſk ye,
Which of ye all could hold from?

   Luc. I perceive ye,
Your own dark Sins dwell with ye, and that Price
You sell the Chaſtity of modeſt Wives at,
Run to Diſeaſes with your Bones: I scorn ye,
And all the Nets ye have pitch'd to catch my Virtues,
Like Spiders Webs, I sweep away before me.
Go, tell the Emperor, ye have met a Woman,
That neither his own Perſon, which is God-like,
The World he rules, nor what that World can purchaſe,
Nor all the Glories subject to a *Cæſar,*
The Honours that he offers for my Body,
The Hopes, Gifts, everlaſting Flatteries,
Nor any thing that's his, and apt to tempt me,
No, not to be the Mother of the Empire,

B

And

And Queen of all the holy Fires he worships,
Can make a Whore of.

Ard. You miſtake us, Lady.

Luc. Yet, tell him this has thus much weaken'd me,
That I have here his Knaves, and you his Matrons,
Fit Nurſes for his Sins, which Gods forgive me,
But ever to be leaning to his Folly,
Or to be brought to love his Luſt, aſſure him,
And from her Mouth, whoſe Life ſhall make it certain,
I never can: I have a Noble Husband,
Pray tell him that too, yet a Noble Name,
A Noble Family, and laſt a Conſcience:
Thus much for your Anſwer: For your ſelves,
You have liv'd the Shame of Women, die the better.   [*Exit.*

Phor. What's now to do?

Ard. Even as ſhe ſaid, to die,
For there's no living here, and Women thus,
I am ſure for us two.

Phor. Nothing ſtick upon her?

Ard. We have loſt a Maſs of Mony; well, Dame Virtue,
Yet ye may halt, if good Luck ſerve.

Phor. Worms take her,
She has almoſt ſpoil'd our Trade.

Ard. So Godly!
This is ill Breeding, *Phorba.*

Phor. If the Women
Shou'd have a longing now to ſee this Monſter,
And ſhe Convert 'em all!

Ard. That may be, *Phorba*;
But if it be, I'll have the young Men gelded:
Come, let's go think, ſhe muſt not 'ſcape us thus;
There is a certain Seaſon, if we hit,
That Women may be rid without a Bit.   [*Exeunt.*

SCENE III.

Enter Maximus *and* Æcius.

Max. I cannot blame the Nations, noble Friend,
That they fall off ſo faſt from this wild Man,
When (under our Allegiance be it ſpoken,
And the moſt happy tye of our Affections)
The World's Weight groans beneath him; where lives Virtue,
Honour, Diſcretion, Wiſdom? Who are clad,
And choſen to the ſteering of the Empire,
But Bawds, and ſinging Girls? O my *Æcius*!
The Glory of a Soldier, and the Truth

Of

Of Men made up for goodneſs ſake, like Shells,
Grow to the ragged Walls for want of Action
Only your happy ſelf, and I that love ye,
Which is a larger Means to me than Favour.

Æcius. No more, my worthy Friend, though theſe be Truths,
And though theſe Truths would ask a Reformation,
At leaſt, a little ſquaring; yet remember
We are but Subjects, *Maximus*; Obedience
To what is done, and Grief for what is ill done,
Is all we can call ours: The Hearts of Princes
Are like the Temples of the Gods; pure Incence,
Until unhallowed Hands defile thoſe Offerings,
Burns ever there; we muſt not put 'em out,
Becauſe the Prieſts that touch thoſe Sweets are wicked;
We dare not, deareſt Friend, nay more we cannot,
While we conſider why we are, and how,
To what Laws bound, much more to what Law-giver;
Whilſt Majeſty is made to be obey'd,
And not inquir'd into, whilſt Gods and Angels
Make but a Rule as we do, though a ſtricter;
Like deſperate and unſeaſon'd Fools, let fly
Our killing Angers, and forſake our Honours.

Max My Noble Friend, from whoſe Inſtructions
I never yet took Surfeit, weigh but thus much,
Nor think I ſpeak it with Ambition,
For by the Gods I do not; why *Æcius*,
Why are we thus, or how become thus wretched?

Æcius. You'll fall again into your Fit.

Max. I will not.
Or are we now no more the Sons of *Romans*,
No more the followers of their happy Fortunes,
But conquer'd *Gauls*, or Quivers for the *Parthians*?
Why is this Emperor, this Man we honour,
This God that ought to be——

Æci You are too curious.

Max. Good, give me leave, why is this Author of us——

Æci. I dare not hear ye ſpeak thus.

Max I'll be modeſt;
Thus led away, thus vainly led away,
And we Beholders? miſconceive me not,
I ſow no Danger in my Words; but wherefore,
And to what end, are we the Sons of Fathers
Famous, and faſt to *Rome*? Why are their Virtues
Stamp'd in the Dangers of a thouſand Battels
For goodneſs ſake; their Honours, time out daring?
I think for our Example.

Æci

Æci. Ye speak nobly.

Max. Why are we Seeds of these then, to shake Hands
With Bawds and base Informers, kiss Discredit,
And court her like a Mistress? Pray, your leave yet;
You'll say the Emperor is young, and apt
To take Impression rather from his Pleasures,
Than any constant Worthiness; it may be.
But, why do these, the People call his Pleasures,
Exceed the Moderation of a Man?
Nay, to say justly Friend, why are they Vices,
And such as shake our Worths with Foreign Nations?

Æci. You search the Sore too deep, and I must tell ye,
In any other Man this had been boldness,
And so rewarded, pray depress your Spirit;
For though I constantly believe ye honest,
Ye were no Friend for me else, and what now
Ye freely spake, but good ye owe to th' Empire;
Yet take heed, worthy *Maximus*, all Ears
Hear not with that Distinction mine do; few
You'll find Admonishers, but Urgers of your Actions,
And to the heaviest, Friend; and pray consider,
We are but Shadows, Motions others give us;
And though our Pities may become the Times,
Justly our Powers cannot; make me worthy
To be your ever Friend in fair Allegiance,
But not in Force: For, durst mine own Soul urge me
(And by that Soul, I speak my just Affections)
To turn my Hand from Truth, which is Obedience,
And give the Helm my Virtue holds, to Anger,
Though I had both the blessings of the *Brutii*,
And both their Instigations, though my Cause
Carried a Face of Justice beyond theirs,
And as I am a Servant to my Fortunes,
That daring Soul, that first taught Disobedience,
Should feel the first Example: Say the Prince,
As I may well believe, seems vitious,
Who justly knows 'tis not to try our Honours?
Or say, he be an ill Prince, are we therefore
Fit Fires to purge him? No, my dearest Friend,
The Elephant is never won with Anger,
Nor must that Man that would reclaim a Lion,
Take him by th' Teeth.

Max. I pray mistake me not.

Æci. Our honest Actions, and the Light that breaks
Like Morning from our Service, chaste and blushing,
Is that that pulls a Prince back; then he sees,
And not till then truly repents his Errors,

When

When Subjects Chryftal Souls are Glaff.s to him :
Max. My ever honour'd Friend, I'll take your Counfel :
The Emperor appears, I'll leave ye to him,
And as we both affect him, may he flourifh.   [*Exit.*
          Enter the Emperor and Chilax.
  Emp. Is that the beft News?
  Chi. Yet the beft we know, Sir.
  Emp. Bid *Maximus* come to me, and be gone then:
Mine own Head by my helper, thefe are Fools.
How now, *Æcius,* are the Soldiers quiet?
  Æci. Better, I hope, Sir, than they were.
  Emp. They are pleas'd, I hear,
To cenfure me extreamly for my Pleafures,
Shortly they'll fight againft me.
  Æci. Gods defend, Sir.
And for their Cenfures, they are fuch fhrewd Judgers,
A Donative of ten Sefterties
I'll undertake fhall make 'em ring your Praifes,
More than they fang your Pleafurers.
  Emp. I believe thee.
Art thou in Love, *Æcius,* yet?
  Æci. O no Sir !
I am too courfe for Ladies ; my Embraces,
That only am acquainted with Alarms,
Would break their tender Bodies.
  Emp. Never fear it,
They are ftronger than ye think, they'll hold the Hammer,
My Emprefs fwears thou art a lufty Soldier,
A good one I believe thee.
  Æci. All that Goodnefs
Is but your Grace's Creature.
  Emp. Tell me truly,
For thou dar'ft tell me.
  Æci. Any thing concerns ye,
That's fit for me to fpeak and you to pardon.
  Emp. What fay the Soldiers of me, and the fame Words,.
Mince 'em not, good *Æcius,* but deliver
The very Forms and Tongues they talk withal.
  Æci. I'll tell your Grace, but with this Caution
You be not ftirr'd ; for fhould the Gods live with us,
Even thofe we certainly believe are Righteous,
Give 'em but Drink, they would cenfure them too.
  Emp. Forward.
  Æci. Then to begin, they fay you fleep too much,
By which they judge your Majefty too fenfual,
Apt to decline your Strength to Eafe and Pleafures ;

                                        Then

And when you do not sleep, you drink too much,
From which they fear Suspicions first, then Ruins;
And when ye neither drink nor sleep, ye wench much,
Which they affirm first breaks your Understanding,
Then takes the Edge of Honour, makes us seem,
That are the Ribs and Rampires of the Empire,
Fencers, and beaten Fools, and so regarded:
But I believe 'em not; for were these Truths,
Your Virtue can correct them.

 Emp. They speak plainly.

 Æci. They say moreover (since your Grace will have it,
For they will talk their Freedoms, though the Sword
Were in their Throat) that of late time, like *Nero*,
And with the same forgetfulness of Glory,
You have got a vain of Filing, so they term it.

 Emp. Some drunken Dreams, *Æcius.*

 Æci. So I hope, Sir.
And that you rather study Cruelty,
And to be feared for Blood, than lov'd for Bounty,
Which makes the Nations, as they say, despise ye,
Telling your Years and Actions by their Deaths,
Whose Truth and strength of Duty made you *Cæsar.*
They say besides, you nourish strange Devourers,
Fed with the Fat o' th' Empire, they call Bawds,
Lazy and lustful Creatures that abuse ye,
A People, as they term 'em, made of Paper,
In which the secret Sins of each Man's Monies
Are sealed and sent a working.

 Emp. What Sin's next?
For I perceive they have no mind to spare me.

 Æci. Nor hurt ye, O my Soul, Sir! But such People
(Nor can the Power of Man restrain it)
When they are full of Meat and Ease, must prattle.

 Emp. Forward,

 Æci. I have spoken too much, Sir

 Emp. I'll have all.

 Æci. It fits not
Your Ears should hear their Vanities; no Profit
Can justly rise to you from their Behaviour,
Unless ye were guilty of those Crimes.

 Emp. It may be
I am so, therefore forward.

 Æci. I have ever
Learn'd to obey, nor shall my Life resist it.

 Emp. No more Apologies.

 Æci. They grieve besides, Sir,

To

To see the Nations, whom our ancient Virtue
With many a weary March and Hunger conquer'd,
With loss of many a darling Life subdu'd,
Fall from their fair Obedience, and even murmur
To see the warlike Eagles mew their Honours
In obscure Towns, that wont to prey on Princes;
They cry for Enemies, and tell the Captains
The Fruits of *Italy* are luscious, give us *Ægypt*,
Or sandy *Africk* to display our Valours,
There where our Swords may make us Meat, and Danger
Digest our well-got Vyands. Here our Weapons,
And Bodies that were made for shining Brass,
Are both unedg'd and old with Ease and Women;
And then they cry again, Where are the *Germans*,
Lin'd with hot *Spain*, or *Gallia*, bring 'em on,
And let the Son of War, steel'd *Mithridates*,
Lead up his winged *Parthians* like a Storm,
Hiding the Face of Heav'n with Showers of Arrows;
Yet we dare fight like *Romans*; then, as Soldiers,
Tyr'd with a weary March, they tell their Wounds,
Even weeping ripe, they were no more, nor deeper,
And glory in those Scars that make 'em lovely;
And sitting where a Camp was, like sad Pilgrims,
They reckon up the Times, and living Labours
Of *Julius* or *Germanicus*, and wonder
That *Rome*, whose Turrets once were topt with Honours,
Can now forget the Custom of her Conquests:
And then they blame your Grace, and say, Who leads us?
Shall we stand here like Statues? Were our Fathers
The Sons of lazy *Moors*, our Princes *Persians*,
Nothing but Silks and Softness? Curses on 'em
That first taught *Nero* Wantonness and Blood,
Tiberius Doubts, *Caligula* all Vices;
For from the Spring of these, succeeding Princes——
Thus they talk, Sir.
  Emp. Well,
Why do you hear these Things?
  Æci. Why do you do 'em?
I take the Gods to Witness, with more Sorrow,
And more Vexation, do I hear these Taintures,
Than were my Life dropt from me through an Hour-glass.
  Emp. Belike then you believe 'em, or at least
Are glad they should be so; take heed, you were better
Build your own Tomb, and run into it living,
Than dare a Prince's Anger.
  Æci. I am Old, Sir,

And

And ten Years more addition, is but nothing:
Now if my Life be pleasing to ye, take it,
Upon my Knees, if ever any Service,
As let me brag, some have been worthy notice,
If ever any Worth or Trust ye gave me,
Deserv'd a fair respect, if all my Actions,
The hazards of my Youth, Colds, Burnings, Wants,
For you and for the Empire, be not Vices;
By that stile ye have stampt upon me, Soldier,
Let me not fall into the Hands of Wretches.

 Emp. I understand ye not.

 Æci. Let not this Body,
That has look'd bravely in his Blood for *Cæsar*,
And covetous of Wounds, and for your safety,
After the scape of Swords, Spears, Slings, and Arrows,
'Gainst which my beaten Body was mine Armour,
The Seas, and thirsty Desarts, now be purchase
For Slaves, and base Informers: I see Anger,
And Death look through your Eyes: I am mark'd for slaughter
And know the telling of this Truth has made me
A Man clean lost to this World; I embrace it;
Only my last Petition, Sacred *Cæsar*,
Is, I may dye a *Roman*.

 Emp. Rise my Friend still,
And worthy of my Love; reclaim the Soldier,
I'll study to do so upon my self too;
Go keep your Command, and prosper.

 Æci. Life to *Cæsar*.   [*Exit*

Enter Chilax.

 Chi. Lord *Maximus* attends your Grace.

 Emp. Go tell him,
I'll meet him in the Gallery.
The Honesty of this *Æcius*,
Who is indeed the Bulwark of the Empire,
Has div'd so deep into me, that of all
The Sins I covet, but this Woman's Beauty,
With much Repentance, now I could be quit of:
But she is such a Pleasure, being good,
That though I were a God, she would fire my Blood.

             [*Exit.*

A C T

ACT II. SCENE I.

The Emperor, Maximus, Lycinius, Proculus, *and* Chilax,
as at Dice.

Emp. NAY ye shall set my Hand out, 'tis not just
I should neglect my fortune, now 'tis prosperous.

Lyc If I have any thing to set your Grace,
But Cloaths or good Conditions, let me perish,
You have all my Mony, Sir.

Pro. And mine.

Chi. And mine too.

Max. Unless your Grace will credit us.

Emp No bare Board.

Lyc. Then at my Garden-House.

Emp. The Orchard too.

Lyc. And't please your Grace.

Emp Have at 'em.

Pro. They are lost.

Lyc. Why farewel Fig-trees,

Emp. Who sets more?

Chil. At my Horse, Sir.

Emp. The dapl'd *Spaniard?*

Chil. He.

Emp. He's mine.

Chil. He is so.

Max. Your short Horse is soon curried.

Chil. So it seems, Sir;
So may your Mare be too, if luck serve.

Max. Ha?

Chi Nothing, my Lord, but grieving at my Fortune.

Emp. Come, *Maximus,* you were not wont to flinch thus.

Max. By Heav'n, Sir, I have lost all.

Emp. There's a Ring yet.

Max. This was not made to lose, Sir.

Emp. Some Love Token;
Set it I say.

Max. I do beseech your Grace,
Rather name any House I have.

Emp. How strange,
And curious you are grown of Toys? Redeem't,
If so I win it, when you please, to Morrow,
Or next Day, as ye will, I care not,
But only for my Luck sake: 'Tis not Rings
Can make me richer.

Max. Will you throw, Sir? There 'tis.

C

Emp. Why then have at it fairly: Mine.

Max. Your Grace
Is only ever Fortunate: To Morrow,
An't be your Pleasure, Sir, I'll pay the Price on't.

Emp. To Morrow you shall have it without Price, Sir,
But this Day 'tis my Victory. Good *Maximus*,
Now I bethink my self, go to *Æcius*,
And bid him muster all the Cohorts presently;
They mutiny for Pay I hear, and be you
Assistant to him; when you know their Numbers,
Ye shall have Monies for 'em, and above
Something to stop their Tongues withal.

Max. I will, Sir:
And Gods preserve you in this Mind still.

Emp. Shortly I'll see 'em march my self.

Max. Gods ever keep ye.   [*Exit.*

Emp. To what end do you think this Ring shall serve now?
For you are Fellows only know by rote,
As Birds record their Lessons.

Chi. For the Lady.

Emp. But how for her?

Chi. That I confess I know not.

Emp. Then pray for him that do's: Fetch me an Eunuch
That never saw her yet; and you two see   [*Exit Chil.*
The Court made like a Paradise.

Lyc. We will, Sir.

Emp. Full of fair Shews and Musicks; all your Arts
(As I shall give Instructions) screw to th' highest,
For my main Piece is now a doing: And for fear
You should not take, I'll have another Engine,
Such as if Virtue be not only in her,
She shall not chuse but lean to, let the Women
Put on a graver shew of Welcome.

Pro Well, Sir.

Emp. They are a thought too eager.
                Enter Chilax *and* Lycias *the Eunuch.*

Chi. Here's the Eunuch.

Eun. Long Life to *Cæsar.*

Emp. I must use you, *Lycias:*
Come let's walk in, and then I'll shew ye all:
If Women may be frail, this Wench shall fall.   [*Exeunt.*

SCENE II.

Enter Claudia, *and* Marcellina.

Clau. Sirrah, what ails my Lady, that of late
She never cares for Company?
                                                        Mar.

Mar. I know not,
Unless it be that Company causes Cuckolds.
  Clau. That were a childish fear.
  Mar. What were those Ladies
Came to her lately,
From the Court?
  Clau. The same, Wench.
Some grave Instructors on my Life, they look
For all the World like old hatch'd Hilts.
  Mar. 'Tis true, Wench.
For here and there, and yet they painted well too,
One might discover, where the Gold was worn,
Their Iron Ages.
  Clau. If my Judgment fail not,
They have been sheath'd like rotten Ships.
  Mar. It may be.
  Clau. For if ye mark their Rudders, they hang weakly.
  Mar. They have past the Line belike; Would'st live, *Claudia*,
'Till thou wert such as they are?
  Clau. Chimney-pieces.
Now Heav'n have Mercy on me, and young Mer,
I had rather make a drallery 'till thirty,
While I were able to endure a Tempest,
And bear my Fights out bravely, 'till my Tackle
Whistled i'th' Wind, and held against all Weathers,
While I were able to bear with my Tyres,
And so discharge 'em, I would willingly
Live, *Marcellina*, not 'till Barnacles
Bred in my Sides.
  Mar. Thou art i'th' right, Wench:
For who wou'd live, whom Pleasures had forsaken,
To stand at Mark, and cry a Bow short Signeur?
Were there not Men come hither too?
  Clau. Brave Fellows.
I fear me Bawds of five i'th' Pound.
  Mar. How know you?
  Clau. They gave me great Lights to it.
  Mar. Take heed, *Claudia*.
  Clau. Let them take heed, the Spring comes on.
  Mar. To me now,
They seem'd as noble Visitants.
  Clau To me now
Nothing less *Marcellina*, for I mark 'em,
And by this honest Light, for yet 'tis Morning,
Saving the Reverence of their gilded Doublets
And *Millan* Skins.

Mar.

Mar. Thou art a strange Wench, *Claudia.*

Clau. Ye are deceiv'd, they shew'd to me directly
Court Crabbs that creep a side=way for their living,
know 'em by the Breeches that they beg'd last.

Mar. Peace, my Lady comes; what may that be?

  Enter Lucina, *and* Lycias *the Eunuch.*

Clau. A Sumner
That cites to her appear.

Mar. No more of that, Wench.

Eun. Madam, what answer to your Lord?

Luc Pray tell him, I am subject to his Will.

Eun Why weep you, Madam?
Excellent Lady, there are none will hurt you.

Luc. I do beseech you tell me, Sir.

Eun What, Lady?

Luc. Serve ye Emperor?

Eun I do.

Luc. In what Place?

Eun In's Chamber, Madam.

Luc. Do you serve his Will too?

Eun. In fair and just Commands.

Luc. Are ye a *Roman?*

Eun. Yes noble Lady, and a *Mantuan.*

Luc. What Office bore your Parents?

Eun One was Pretor.

Luc. Take then heed how you stain his Reputation.

Eun. Why, worthy Lady?

Luc. If ye know, I charge ye,
Ought in this Message, but what Honesty,
The Trust and fair Obedience of a Servant,
May well deliver, yet take heed, and help me.

Eun Madam, I am no Broker.

Clau I'll be hang'd then.

Eun Nor base Procurer of Mens Lusts; Your Husband
Pray'd me to do this Office, I have done it,
It rests in you to come, or no.

Luc I will, Sir.

Eun. If ye mistrust me, do not.

Luc Ye appear so worthy,
And to all my Sense so honest,
And this is such a certain sign ye have brought me,
That I believe.

Eun Why should I cozen you?
Or were I brib'd to do this Villany,
Can Money prosper, or the Fool that takes it,
When such a Virtue falls?

            Luc.

Luc. Ye speak well, Sir;
Wou'd all the rest that serve the Emperor
Had but your way.
   Clau. And so they have *ad unguem.*
   Luc Pray tell my Lord, I have receiv'd his Token,
And will not fail to meet him; yet, good Sir, thus much
Before you go, I do beseech ye too,
As little notice as ye can, deliver
Of my Appearance there.
   Eun. It shall be, Madam,
And so I wish you Happiness.
   Luc. I thank you.   [*Exeunt.*

SCENE III.

Tumult and Noise within. Enter Æcius *pursuing* Pontius *the Captain, and* Maximus *following.*

   Max. Temper your self, *Æcius.*
  Pon Hold, my Lord.
I am a *Roman*, and a Soldier.
   Max. Pray, Sir.
   Æci Thou art a lying Villain, and a Traitor;
Give me my self, or by the Gods, my Friend,
You'll make me dangerous; how du'st thou pluck
The Soldiers to Sedition, and I living,
And sow Rebellion in 'em, and even then
When I am drawing out to action?
   Pon. Hear me.
   Max. Are ye a Man?
   Æci. I am a true hearted, *Maximus,*
And if the Villain live, we are dishonour'd.
   Max. But hear him what he can say.
   Æci. That's the way
To pardon him; I am so easie-natur'd,
That if he speak but humbly I forgive him.
   Pon I do beseech ye, noble General.
   Æci H as found the way already; give me room,
One stroke, and if he scape me then, h'as Mercy.
   Pon. I do not call ye Noble, that I fear ye,
I never car'd for Death; if ye will kill me,
Consider first for what, not what you can do;
'Tis true, I know ye for my General,
And by that great Prerogative may kill:
But do it justly then
   Æci. He argues with me:
By Heav'n a made up Rebel.
   Max. Pray consider,

                             W hat

What certain grounds ye have for this.

Æci. What grounds?

Did I not take him preaching to the Soldiers
How lazily they liv'd, and what Dishonours
It was to serve a Prince so full of Woman?
Those were his very words, Friend.

Max. These, *Æcius,*
Though they were rashly spoke, which was an Error
(A great one, *Pontius*) yet from him that hungers
For Wars, and brave Imployment, might be pardon'd.
The Heart, and harbour'd Thoughts of Ill, make Traitors,
Not spleeny Speeches. *Æci.* Why should you protect him?
Go too, it shews not honest. *Max.* Taint me not,
For that shews worse, *Æcius:* All your Friendship,
And that pretended Love ye lay upon me,
Hold back my Honesty, is like a Favour
You do your Slave to day, to morrow hang him.
Was I your Bosom-piece for this? *Æci.* Forgive me;
The Nature of my Zeal, and for my Country,
Makes me sometimes forget my self; for know,
Though I must strive to be without my Passions,
I am no God. For you, Sir, whose Infection
Has spread it self like Poison through the Army,
And cast a killing fog on fair Allegiance,
First thank this noble Gentleman, ye had dy'd else.
Next from your Place, and honour of a Soldier,
I here seclude you. *Pon.* May I speak yet? *Max.* Hear him.

Æci And while *Æcius* holds a Reputation,
At least Command, ye bear no Arms for *Rome,* Sir.

Pon. Against her I shall never: The condemn'd Man
Has yet that privilege to speak, my Lord;
Law were not equal else. *Max.* Pray hear, *Æcius;*
For happily the fault he has committed,
Though I believe it mighty, yet consider'd,
If Mercy may be thought upon, will prove
Rather a hasty Sin, than heinous. *Æci* Speak.

Pon 'Tis true, my Lord, ye took me tyr'd with Peace,
My Words almost as ragged as my Fortunes:
'Tis true, I told the Soldier whom we serv'd,
And then bewail'd, we had an Emperor
Led from us by the flourishes of Fencers;
I blam'd him too for Women. *Æci.* To the rest, Sir.

Pon. And like enough, I blest him then as Soldiers
Will do sometimes: 'Tis true I told 'em too,
We lay at Home, to shew our Country
We durst go naked, durst want Meat, and Mony;

And

And when the Slave drinks Wine, we durft be thirfty:
I told 'em this too, that the Trees and Roots
Were our beft Pay-mafters; the Charity
Of longing Women, that had bought our Bodies,
Our Beds, Fires, Taylors, Nurfes; nay, I told 'em,
(For you fhall hear the greateft Sin, I faid, Sir)
By that time there be Wars again, our Bodies,
Laden with Scars and Aches, and ill Lodgings,
Heats, and perpetual Wants, were fitter Prayers,
And certain Graves, than cope the Foe on Crutches:
'Tis likely too, I counfel'd 'em to turn
Their warlike Pikes to Plough-fhares, their fure Targets
And Swords hatch'd with the Blood of many Nations,
To Spades, and pruning Knives, for thefe get Mony,
Their warlike Eagles, into Daws, or Starlings,
To give an *Ave Cafar* as he paffes,
And be rewarded with a thoufand Drachma's:
For thus we get but Years and Beets. 　*Æci.* What think you,
Were thefe Words to be fpoken by a Captain,
One that fhould give Example? 　*Max.* 'Twas too much.
　Pon. My Lord, I did not wooe 'em from the Empire,
Nor bid 'em turn their daring Steel 'gainft *Cafar*;
The Gods for ever hate me, if that Motion
Were part of me · Give me but Imployment, Sir,
And way to live, and where you hold me vicious,
Bred up in Mutiny; my Sword fhall tell ye,
And if you pleafe, that Place I held, maintain it,
'Gainft the moft daring Foes of *Rome*, I am honeft,
A lover of my Country, one that holds
His Life no longer his, than kept for *Cafar.*
Weigh not (I thus low on my Knee befeech you)
What my rude Tongue difcover'd, 'twas my Want,
No other part of *Pontius* : You have feen me,
And you, my Lord, do fomething for my Country,
And both beheld the Wounds I gave and took,
Not like a backward Traitor. 　*Æci.* All this Language
Makes but againft you, *Pontius,* you are caft,
And by mine Honour, and my Love to *Cafar*,
By me fhall never be reftored; in my Camp
I will not have a Tongue, though to himfelf,
Dare talk but near Sedition; as I govern,
All fhall obey; and when they want, their Duty
And ready Service fhall redrefs their Needs,
Not prating what they would be. 　*Pon.* Thus I leave ye,
Yet fhall my Prayers ftill, although my Fortunes
Muft follow you no more, be ftill about ye,

　　　　　　　　　　　　　　　　　　　Gods

Gods give ye where ye fight the Victory,
Ye cannot caſt my Wiſhes. *Æci.* Come my Lord,
Now to the Field again. *Max.* Alas poor *Pontius!* [*Exeunt.*

SCENE IV.

Enter Chilax *at one Door,* Lycinius *and* Balbus *at another.*

Ly. How now? *Chi.* She's come.
Bal. Then I'll to the Emperor. [*Exit.*
Chi Do, Is the Muſick placed well? *Lyc.* Excellent.
Chi Lycinius, you ard *Proculus* receive her
In the great Chamber, at her Entrance,
Let me alone, and do you hear *Lycinius,*
Pray 'et the Ladies ply her further off,
And with much more Diſcretion. One Word more.
Lc Well
Chi. Are the Jewels, and thoſe ropes of Pearl,
Laid in the way ſhe paſſes?

Enter Emperor, Balbus *and* Proculus.

Lyc Take no care, Man. [*Ex. Lyc.*
Emp. What, is ſhe come? *Chi.* She is, Sir; but 'twere beſt
Your Grace were ſeen laſt to her. *Emp* So I mean;
Keep the Court empty, *Proculus.* *Pro.* 'Tis done, Sir.
Emp Be not too ſudden to her. *Chi* Good your Grace
Retire, and Man your ſelf; let us alone
We are no Children this way: Do you hear, Sir?
'Tis neceſſary that her Waiting-women
Be cut off in the Lobby, by ſome Ladies,
They'd break the buſineſs elſe. *Emp* 'Tis true, they ſhall.
Chi Remember your place, *Proculus.*
Pro I warrant ye. [*Exeunt* Emp. Balb. *and* Pro.
Enter Lucina, Claudia, *and* Marcellina.
Chi She enters; Who are Waitors there? The Emperor
Calls for his Horſe to air himſelf. *Luc.* I am glad
I come ſo happily to take him abſent,
This takes away a little fear; I know him,
Now I begin to fear again: Oh Honour,
If ever thou hadſt Temple in weak Woman,
And Sacrifice of Modeſty burnt to thee,
Hold me faſt now, and help me. *Chi.* Noble Madam,
Ye are welcome to the Court, moſt nobly welcome,
Ye are a Stranger, Lady. *Luc.* I deſire ſo.
Chi A wondrous Stranger here, nothing ſo ſtrange:
And therefore need a Guide, I think. *Luc.* I do, Si,
And that a good one too. *Chi.* My Service, Lady,
Shall be your Guard in this Place: But pray ye tell me,

Are

Are ye refolv'd a Courtier?   *Luc.* No, I hope, Sir.

    Clau. You are, Sir.   *Chi.* Yes, my fair one.   *Clau.* So it feems,
You are fo ready to beftow your felf.
Pray what might coft thofe Breeches?

    Chi. Would you weai 'em?
Madam, ye have a Witty Woman.   *Mar.* Two, Sir,
Or elfe ye underbuy us.   *Luc.* Leave your talking:
But is my Lord here, I befeech ye, Sir?

    Chi. He is, fweet Lady, and muft take this kindly,
Exceeding kindly of ye, wondious kindly,
Ye come fo far to vifit him: I'll guide ye.

    Luc. Whither?   *Chi.* Why, to your Lord.   *Luc.* Is it fo hard, Sir,
To find him in this place without a Guide?
For I would willingly not trouble you.

    Chi. It will be fo foi you that are a Stranger;
Nor can it be a trouble to do fervice
To fuch a worthy Beauty, and befide ——

    Mar. I fee he will go with us.   *Clau.* Let him amble.

    Chi. It fits not that a Lady of your reckoning,
Should pafs without Attendants.   *Luc.* I have twe, Sir.

    Chi. I mean without a Man: You'll fee the Emperor?

    Luc. Alas, I am not fit, Sir.   *Chi.* You are well enough;
He'll take it wondious kindly: Hark.   *Luc.* Ye flatter;
Good Sir, no more of that.   *Chi.* Well, I but tell ye.

    Luc. Will ye go forward; fince I muft be Man'd,
Pray take your Place.   *Clau.* Cannot ye Man us too, Sir?

    Chi. Give me but time.   *Mar.* And you'll try all things?

    Chi. No, I'll make ye no fuch promife.   *Claud.* If ye do, Sir,
Take heed ye ftand to't.   *Chi.* Wondrous merry Ladies.

    Luc. The Wenches are difpos'd, pray keep your way, Sir [*Exeunt.*

       Enter Lycinius, Proculus, *and* Balbus.

    Lyc. She is coming up the Stairs; Now the Mufick;
And as that ftirs her, let's fet on: Perfumes there.

    Pro. Difcover all the Jewels.   *Lyc.* Peace.   [*Mufick.*

S O N G S.

Now the lufty Spring is feen,
   Golden Yellow, gaudy Blue,
   Daintily invite the View
Every where, on every Green,
   Rofes blufhing as they blow,
     And inticing Men to pull,
   Lillies whiter than the Snow,
Woodbines of fweet Honey full.

     D   *All*

All Love's Emblems, and all cry,
Ladies, if not pluck'd we die.

Yet the lusty Spring hath staid,
  Blushing red and purest White,
  Daintily to Love invite,
Every Woman, every Maid;
Cherries kissing as they grow,
  And inviting Men to taste,
Apples even ripe below,
  Winding gently to the waste,
    All Love's Emblems and all cry,
    Ladies, if not pluck'd we die.

SECOND.

Hear ye, Ladies, that despise,
  What the mighty Love has done,
Fear Examples, and be wise,
  Fair Calisto was a Nun,
Læda sailing on the Stream,
  To deceive the hopes of Man,
Love accounting but a Dream,
  Doated on a silver Swan.
    Danae in a Brazen Tower,
    Where no Love was, lov'd a Shower.

Hear ye Ladies that are coy,
  What the mighty Love can do:
Fear the fierceness of the Boy,
  The chaste Moon he makes to woo:
Vesta kindling holy Fires,
  Circled round about with Spies,
Never dreaming loose Desires,
  Doating at the Altar dies.
    Ilion in a short Hour higher,
    He can build, and once more fire.

Enter Chilax, Lucina, Claudia, *and* Marcellina.
Luc. Pray Heav'n my Lord be here, for now I fear it.
Well Ring, if thou bee't counterfeit, or stol'n,
As by this Preparation I suspect it,
Thou hast betray'd thy Mistress: Pray, Sir, forward,
I would fain see my Lord.   *Chi.* But tell me, Madam,
How do ye like the Song?   *Luc.* I like the Air well,
But for the Words, they are lascivious,
And over-light for Ladies.   *Chi* All ours love 'em.
  Luc 'Tis like enough, for yours are loving Ladies.
  Lyc. Madam, ye are welcome to the Court.   Who waits?
                                      Attendants

Attendants for this Lady.   *Luc.* Ye miftake, Sir;
I bring no Triumph with me.   *Lyc.* But much Honour.
  Pro. Why this was nobly done, and like a Neighbour;
So freely of your felf to be a Vifitant,
The Emperor fhall give ye thanks for this.   *Luc.* O no, Sir;
There's nothing to deferve 'em.   *Pro.* Yes, your Prefence.
  Luc. Good Gentlemen be patient, and believe
I come to fee my Husband, on Command too,
I were no Courtier elfe.   *Lyc.* That's all one, Lady,
Now ye are here, you're welcome; and the Emperor,
Who loves ye but too well——   *Luc.* No more of that, Sir,
I came not to be Catechiz'd.   *Pro* Ah, Sirrah;
And have we got you here? faith, Noble Lady,
We'll keep ye one Month Courtier.   *Luc.* Gods defend, Sir,
I never lik'd a Trade worfe.   *Pro.* Hark ye.   *Luc.* No, Sir.
  Pro Ye are grown the ftrangeft Lady. *Luc.* How? *Pro.* By Heav'n,
'Tis true I tell ye, and you'll find it.   *Luc.* I?
I'll rather find my Grave, and fo inform him.
  Pro. Is it not pity, Gentlemen, this Lady
(Nay I'll deal roughly with ye, yet not hurt ye)
Should live alone, and give fuch heav'nly Beauty
Only to Walls and Hangings?   *Luc.* Good Sir, Patience:
I am no Wonder, neither come to that end,
Ye do my Lord an injury to ftay me,
Who, though you are the Prince's, yet dare tell ye,
He keeps no Wife for your ways.   *Bal.* Well, well, Lady;
However you are pleas'd to think of us,
Ye are welcome, and ye fhall be welcome.   *Luc.* Shew it
In that I come for then, in leading me
Where my lov'd Lord is, not in ffattery: [*Jewels fhew'd.*
Nay ye may draw the Curtain, I have feen 'em,
But none worth half my Honefty.   *Clau.* Are thefe, Sir,
Laid here to take?   *Pro.* Yes, for your Lady, Gentlewomen.
  Mar. We had been doing elfe.   *Bal.* Meaner Jewels
Would fit your Worths.   *Clau.* And meaner Cloaths your Bodies.
  Luc. The Gods fhall kill me firft.   *Lyc.* There's better dying
I'th' Emperor's Arms; go to, but be not angry——
Thefe are but Talks, fweet Lady.
            Enter Phorba *and* Ardelia.
  Phor. Where is this Stranger? Rufhes, Ladies, Rufhes;
Rufhes as green as Summer for this Stranger.
  Pro. Here's Ladies come to fee you.   *Luc.* You are gone then?
I take it 'tis your *Cue.*   *Pro.* Or rather Manners;
You are better fitted, Madam, we but tire ye,
Therefore we'll leave ye for an Hour, and bring
Your much lov'd Lord unto you.   [*Exeunt*

Luc. **Then I'll thank ye.**
I am Betray'd for certain; well *Lucina*,
If thou do'st fall from Virtue, may the Earth,
That after Death should shoot up Gardens of thee
Spreading thy living Goodness into Branches,
Fly from thee, and the hot Sun find thy Vices.
   Phor. You are a welcome Woman.   *Ard.* Bless me Heav'n,
How did you find the way to Court?   *Luc.* I know not;
Would I had never trod it.   *Phor* Prithee tell me,
Good noble Lady, and good sweet Heart love us,
For we love thee extreamly; is not this Place
A Paradice to live in?   *Luc.* To those People
That know no other Paradice but Pleasure;
That little I enjoy contents me better.
   Ard. What, heard ye any Musick yet?   *Luc.* Too much.
   Phor. You must not be thus froward; what, this Gown
Is one o'th' prettiest by my Troth, *Ardelia*,
I ever saw yet; 'twas not to frown in, Lady,
Ye put this Gown on when ye came.   *Ard.* How do ye?
Alas poor Wretch, how cold it is!   *Luc.* Content ye;
I am as well as may be, and as temperate,
If ye will let me be so: Where's my Lord?
For there's the business that I came for, Ladies.
   Phor. We'll lead ye to him, he's i'th' Gallery.
   Ard. We'll shew ye all the Court too.   *Luc.* Shew me him,
And ye have shew'd me all I come to look on.
   Phor Come on, we'll be your Guides, and as ye go,
We have some pretty Tales to tell ye, Lady,
Shall make ye merry too; ye come not here,
To be a sad *Lucina.*   *Luc.* Would I might not.   *[Exeunt.*
       Enter Chilax *and* Balbus.
  Chi Now the soft Musick; *Balbus* run.
  Bal I fly, Boy.   *[Exit* Balbus.
  Chi. The Women by this time are worming of her,——
If she can hold out them, the Emperor   *[Musick.*
Takes her to task: He has her; hark the Musick.
       Enter Emperor *and* Lucina.
  Luc Good your Grace,
Where are my Women, Sir?
  Emp They are wise, beholding
What you think scorn to look on, the Court's Bravery:
Would you have run away so slily, Lady,
And not have seen me?   *Luc.* I beseech your Majesty,
Consider what I am, and whose.   *Emp.* I do so.
  Luc. Believe me, I shall never make a Whore, Sir.
  Emp. A Friend ye may, and to that Man that loves ye,
More than you love your Virtue.   *Luc.* Sacred *Cæsar.*

                              Emp.

Emp. You fhall not kneel to me, Sweet. *Luc.* Look upon me,
And if ye be fo cruel to abufe me,
Think how the Gods will take it ; Does this Beauty
Afflict your Soul ? I'll hide it from you ever,
Nay more, I will become fo leprous,
That ye fhall curfe me from ye: My dear Lord
Has ferv'd ye ever truly, fought your Battels,
As if he daily long'd to dye for *Cæfar* ;
Was never Traitor, Sir, nor never tainted
In all the Actions of his Life. *Emp.* I know it.
   Luc. His Fame and Family have grown together,
And fpread together like to failing Cedars,
Over the *Roman* Diadem ; oh let not,
As ye have any Flefh that's human in you,
The having of a modeft Wife decline him,
Let not my Virtue be the Wedge to break him ;
I do not think ye are lafcivious,
Thefe wanton Men belye ye, you are *Cæfar*,
Which is the Father of the Empire's Honour,
Ye are too near the Nature of the Gods,
To wrong the weakeft of all Creatures, Women.
   Emp. I dare not do it here. Rife fair *Lucina*,
I did but try your Temper, ye are honeft,
And with the Commendations wait on that
I'll lead ye to your Lord, and ye to him:
Wipe your fair Eyes: He that endeavours Ill,
May well delay, but never quench his Hell.   [*Exeunt.*

ACT III. SCENE I.

Enter Chilax, Lycinius, Proculus, *and* Balbus.

Chi. 'TIS done, *Lycinius.* *Lyc.* How ? *Chi.* I fhame to tell it ;
         If there be any Juftice, we are Villains,
And muft be fo rewarded. *Bal.* If it be done,
I take it 'tis no time now to Repent it ;
Let's make the beft o'th' Trade. *Pro.* Now Veng'ance take it.
Why fhould not he have fettled on a Beauty,
Whofe Honefty ftuck in a piece of Tiffue,
Or one a Ring might iu'e, or fuch a one
That had an itching Husband to be honourable,
And Ground to get it: If he muft have Women,
And no allay without 'em, why not thofe
That know the Mifery, and are beft able
To play again with Judgment? Such as fhe is,
Grant they be won with long Seige, endlefs Travel,
And brought to Opportunity with Millions,

Yet

Yet when they come to Motion, their cold Virtue
Keeps 'em like Cakes of Ice ; I ll melt a Chriftal,
And make a dead Flint fire himfelf, e'er they
Give greater Heat, than now departing Embers
Give to old Men that watch 'em.   *Lyc.* A good **Whore**
Had fav'd all this, and happily as wholfome ;
Ay, and the thing once done too, as well thought of ;
But this fame Chaftity forfooth.   *Pro.* A Pox on't.
Why fhould not Women be as free as we are ?
They are, but not in open, and far free'r,
And the more bold ye bear your felf, more Welcome,
And there is nothing ye dare fay, but Truth,
But they dare hear.
                    Enter Emperor and Lucina.
  Chi. The Emperor ! Away,
And if we can repent, let's Home and pray.   [*Exeunt.*
  Emp. Your only Virtue now is Patience,
Take heed, and fave your Honour ; if you talk ——
  Luc. As long as there is Motion in my Body,
And Life to give me Words, I'll cry for Juftice.
  Emp. Juftice fhall never hear ye, I am Juftice.
  Luc. Wilt thou not kill me, Monfter, Ravifher,
Thou bitter Bane o'th' Empire, look upon me,
And if thy guilty Eyes dare fee thefe Ruins,
Thy wild Luft hath laid level with Difhonour,
The Sacrilegious Razing of this Temple,
The Mother of thy black Sins would have blufh'd at ;
Behold and Curfe thy felf ; the Gods will find thee,
That's all my Refuge now, for they are Righteous.
Vengeance and Horror circle thee ; the Empire,
In which thou liv'ft a ftrong continued Surfeit,
Like Poifon will difgorge thee, good Men raze thee
For ever being read again, —— but Vicious
Women, and fearful Maids, make Vows againft thee ;
Thy own Slaves, if they hear of this, fhall hate thee ;
And thofe thou haft corrupted firft fall from thee ;
And if thou let'ft me live, the Soldier,
Tyr'd with thy Tyrannies, break through Obedience,
And fhake his ftrong Steel at thee.   *Emp.* This prevails not ;
Nor any Agony ye utter, Lady.
If I have done a Sin, curfe her that drew me,
Curfe the firft Caufe, the Witchcraft that abus'd me,
Curfe thofe fair Eyes, and curfe that heav'nly Beauty,
And curfe your being Good too.   *Luc.* Glorious Thief,
What Reftitution can'ft thou make to fave me ?
  Emp. I'll ever Love, and Honour you.   *Luc.* Thou can'ft not,
                                                        For

For that which was mine Honour, thou haft murder'd,
And can there be a Love in Violence?

Emp. You fhall be only mine. *Luc.* Yet I like better
Thy Villany, than Flattery, that's thine own,
The other bafely counterfeit; fly from me,
Or for thy Safety fake and Wifdom kill me,
For I am worfe than thou art; thou may'ft pray,
And fo recover Grace; I am loft for ever,
And if thou let'ft me live, th'art loft thy felf too.

Emp. I fear no Lofs but Love, I ftand above it.

Luc. Call in your Lady Bawds, and gilled Pandars,
And let them triumph too, and fing to *Cæfar,*
Lucina's fallen. the chaft *Lucina*'s conquer'd.
Gods, what a wretched Thing has this Man made me?
For I am now no Wife for *Maximus,*
No Company for Women that are virtuous,
No Family I now can claim, nor Country,
Nor Name, but *Cæfar*'s Whore. O facred *Cæfar,*
(For that fhould be your Title) was your Empire,
Your Rods, and Axes, that are Tipes of Juftice,
Thofe Fires that ever burn, to beg you Bleffings,
The Peoples Adoration, Fear of Nations,
What Victory can bring ye Home, what elfe
The ufeful Elements can make your Servants,
Even Light it felf, and Suns of Light, Truth, Juftice,
Mercy, and Starlike Piety, fent to you,
And from the Gods themfelves, to ravifh Women?
The Curfes that I owe to Enemies,
Even thofe the *Sabines* fent, when *Romulus*
(As thou haft me) ravifh'd ther noble Maids,
Made more, and heavier, light on thee. *Emp.* This helps not.

Luc. The Sins of *Tarquin* be remember'd in thee,
And where there has a chafte Wife been abus'd,
Let it be thine, the Shame thine. thine the Slaughter,
And laft for ever, thine, the fear'd Example
Where fhall poor Virtue live, now I am fall'n?
What can your Honours now, and Empire make me,
But a more glorious Whore? *Emp.* A better Woman:
But if ye will be blind, and fcorn it, who can help it?
Come leave thefe Lamentations, they do nothing
Put make a Noife, I am the fame Man ftill,
Were it to do again; therefore be wifer,
By all this holy Light, I fhould attempt it,
Ye are fo Excellent, and made to ravifh,
There were no Pleafure in you elfe. *Luc.* Oh Villain!

Emp. So bred for Man's amazement, that my Reafon

And

And every help to hold me right has loft me ;
The God of Love himfelf had been before me,
Had he but Power to fee ye ; tell me juftly,
How can I chufe but Err then? If ye dare,
Be mine, and only mine, for ye are fo precious,
I envy any other fhould enjoy ye,
Almoft look on ye, and your daring Husband
Shall know h' as kept an Off'ring from the Empire,
Too Holy for his Altars ; be the mightieft,
More than my felf I'll make it : If ye will not,
Sit down with this, and filence, for which Wifdom
Ye fhall have Ufe of me, and much Honour ever,
And be the fame you were ; if ye divulge it.
Know I am far above the Faults I do,
And thofe I do, I am able to forgive too ;
And where your Credit in the Knowledge of it,
May be with Glofs enough fufpected, mine
Is as mine own Command fhall make it : Princes,
Though they be fometime fubject to loofe Whifpers,
Yet wear they two-edg'd Swords for open Cenfures :
Your Husband cannot help ye, nor the Soldier ;
Your Husband is my Creature, they my Weapons,
And only where I bid 'em, ftrike ; I feed 'em.
Nor can the Gods be angry at this Action,
For as they make me moft, they mean me happieft,
Which I had never been without this Pleafure :
Confider, and farewel : You'll find your Women
At Home before ye, they have had fome Sport too,
But are more thankful for it.   [*Exit Emperor.*

   Luc. Deftruction find thee.
Now which way muft I go? My honeft Houfe
Will fhake to fhelter me, my Husband fly me,
My Family, becaufe they are Honeft, and defire to be fo,
Muft not endure me, not a Neighbour know me :
What Woman now dare fee me without Blufhes,
And pointing as I pafs, There, there, behold her,
Look on her little Children, that is fhe,
That handfome Lady, mark. O my fad Fortunes !
Is this the end of Goodnefs, this the Price
Of all my early Prayers to protect me ?
Why then I fee there is no God but Power,
Nor Virtue now alive that cares for us,
But what is either Lame or Senfual,
How had I been thus wretched elfe ?
                    Enter Maximus *and* Æcius.
   Æci. Let *Titius*

                              Command

Command the Company that *Pontius* loft,
And fee the Foffes deeper. *Max.* How now fweet Heart,
What make you here, and thus? *Æci.* Lucina weeping?
This muft be much Offence. *Max.* Look up and tell me,
Why are you thus? My Ring? O Friend, I have found it!
Ye were at Court, Sweet? *Luc.* Yes, this brought me thither.

   Max. Rife, and go Home : I have my Fears, *Æcius:*
Oh my beft Friend, I am ruin'd; go *Lucina,*
Already in thy Tears, I have read thy Wrongs,
Already found a *Cæfar* ; go thou Lilly,
Thou fweetly drooping Flow'r : Go filver Swan,
And fing thine own fad Requiem: Go *Lucina,*
And if thou dar'ft, out-live this wrong. *Luc.* I dare not.

   Æci. Is that the Ring ye loft? *Max.* That, that, *Æcius,*
That curfed Ring, my felf, and all my Fortunes :
'Thas pleas'd the Emperor, my noble Mafter,
For all my Services, and Dangers for him,
To make me mine own Pandar; was this Juftice ?
Oh my *Æcius,* have I liv'd to bear this ?

   Luc. Farewel for ever, Sir. *Max.* That's a fad faying ;
But fuch a one becomes ye well, *Lucina:*
And yet methinks we fhould not part fo lightly,
Our Loves have been of longer growth, more rooted
Than the fharp Word of one Farewel can fcatter.
Kifs me : I find no *Cæfar* here; thefe Lips
Tafte not of Ravifher in my Opinion.
Was it not fo ? *Luc.* O! Yes. *Max.* I dare believe thee,
For thou wert ever Truth it felf, and Sweetnefs :
Indeed fhe was, *Æcius.* *Æci* So fhe is ftill.

   Max. Once more: O my *Lucina*; O my Comfort,
The Bleffing of my Youth, the Life of my Life.

   Æci. I have feen enough to ftagger my Obedience:
Hold me ye equal Gods, this is too finful.

   Max. Why wert thou chofen out to make a Whore of?
To me thou wert too chafte: Fall Chriftal Fountains,
And ever feed your Streams you rifing Sorrows,
Till you have dropt your Miftrefs into Marble.
Now go for ever from me. *Luc.* Long farewel, Sir.
And as I have been Loyal, Gods think on me.

   Max. Stay, let me once more bid Farewel, *Lucina,*
Farewel thou excellent Example of us,
Thou ftarry Virtue, fare thee well, feek Heav'n,
And there by *Caffiopeia* fhine in Glory,
We are too bafe and dirty to preferve thee.

   Æci. Nay, I muft kifs too: Such a Kifs again,
And from a Woman of fo ripe a Virtue,

E

Ætius must not take: Farewel thou *Phœnix,*
If thou wilt die, *Lucina*; which well weigh'd
If you can cease a while from these strange Thoughts,
I wish were rather alter'd.   *Luc.* No.   *Æti.* Mistake not.
I would not stain your Honour for the Empire,
Nor any way decline you to Discredit,
'Tis not my fair Profession, but a Villain's:
I find and feel your Loss as deep as you do,
And am the same *Ætius*, still as Honest,
The same Life I have still for *Maximus,*
The same Sword wear for you, where Justice wills me,
And 'tis no dull one: Therefore misconceive not:
Only I would have you live a little longer,
But a short Year.   *Max.* She must not.   *Luc.* Why so long, Sir,
Am I not grey enough with Grief already?

  Æti. To draw from that wild Man a sweet Repentance,
And Goodness in his Days to come.   *Max.* They are so,
And will be ever coming, my *Ætius.*

  Æti. For who knows, but the sight of you, presenting
His swoln Sins at the full, and your fair Virtues,
May like a fearful Vision fright his Follies,
And once more bend him right again, which Blessing
(If your dark Wrongs would give you leave to read)
Is more than Death, and the Reward more glorious:
Death only eases you; this, the whole Empire:
Besides compell'd, and forc'd with Violence,
To what ye have done, the Deed is none of yours,
No nor the Justice neither; ye may live,
And still a worthier Woman, still more honour'd:
For are those Trees the worse we tear the Fruits from?
Or should the Eternal Gods desire to perish,
Because we daily violate their Truths,
Which is the Chastity of Heav'n? No, Lady,
If ye dare live, ye may. And as our Sins
Makes them more full of Equity and Justice,
So this compulsive wrong makes you more perfect:
The Empire too will bless ye.   *Max.* Noble Sir,
If she were any thing to me but Honour,
And that that's wedded to me too, laid in,
Not to be worn away without my Being;
Or could the Wrong be hers alone, or mine,
Or both our Wrongs, not ty'd to after Issues,
Not born anew in all our Names and Kindreds,
I would desire her live; nay more, compel her:
But since it was not Youth, but Malice did it;
And not her own, nor mine, but both our Losses,

                                                    Nor

Nor ſtays it there, but that our Names muſt find it
Even thoſe to come; and when they Read, ſhe liv'd,
Muſt they not ask how often ſhe was raviſh'd,
And make a doubt ſhe lov'd that more than Wedlock?
Therefore ſhe muſt not live.   *Æci.* Therefore ſhe muſt live,
To teach the World ſuch Deaths are ſuperſtitious.

   Luc. The Tongues of Angels cannot alter me;
For could the World again reſtore my Credit,
As fair and abſolute as firſt I bred it,
That World I ſhould not truſt again.   The Empire
By my Life can get nothing but my Story,
Which whilſt I breath muſt be but his Abuſes:
And where ye counſel me to live, that *Cæſar*
May ſee his Errors, and repent, I'll tell ye,
His Penitence is but Encreaſe of Pleaſures,
His Prayers never ſaid but to deceive us;
And when he weeps, as you think for his Vices,
'Tis but as killing Drops from baleful Eugh-Trees
That rot their honeſt Neighbour: If he can grieve,
As one that yet deſires his free Converſion,
And almoſt glories in his Penitence,
I'll leave him Robes to mourn in, my ſad Aſhes.

   Æci. The farewels then of happy Souls be with thee,
And to thy Memory be ever ſung
The Praiſes of a juſt and conſtant Lady;
This ſad Day whilſt I live, a Soldier's Tears
I'll offer on thy Monument, and bring
Full of thy noble ſelf with Tears untold yet,
Many a worthy Wife, to weep thy Ruin.

   Max. All that is Chaſt, upon thy Tomb ſhall flouriſh,
All living Epitaphs be thine; Time, Story,
And what is left behind to piece our Lives,
Shall be no more abus'd with Tales and Trifles,
But full of thee, ſtand to Eternity.

   Æci. Once more farewel, go find *Elyſium,*
There where the happy Souls are crown'd with Bleſſings,
There where 'tis ever Spring, and ever Summer.

   Max. There where no bed-rid Juſtice comes; Truth, Honour,
Are Keepers of that bleſſed Place; go thither,
For here thou liveſt chaſt Fire in rotten Timber.

   Æci. And ſo our laſt Farewels.

   Max. Gods give the Juſtice.   [*Exit Lucina.*

   Æci. His Thoughts begin to work; I fear him, yet
He ever was a noble *Roman,* but
I know not what to think on't, he hath ſuffer'd
Beyond a Man, if he ſtand this.   *Max. Æcius,*

E 2   Am

Am I alive, or has a dead Sleep feiz'd me?
It was my Wife the Emperor abus'd thus;
And I muft fay, I am glad I had her for him;
Muft I nor, my *Æcius*?　　　*Æci.* I am ftricken
With fuch a ftiff Amazement, that no Anfwer
Can readily come from me, nor no Comfort:
Will ye go Home, or go to my Houfe?　　*Max.* Neither:
I have no Home, and you are mad *Æcius*
To keep me Company, I am a Fellow
My own Sword would forfake, not ty'd unto me:
A Pander is a Prince, to what I am fallen;
By Heav'n I dare do nothing.　　*Æci.* Ye do better.
　　Max. I am made a branded Slave, *Æcius*,
And yet I blefs the Maker;
Death O' my Soul, muft I endure this tamely?
Muft *Maximus* be mention'd for his Tales?
I am a Child too; what fhould I do railing?
I cannot mend my felf, 'tis *Cæfar* did it,
And what am I to him?　　*Æci.* 'Tis well confider'd;
However you are tainted, be no Traitor,
Time may out-wear the firft, the laft lives ever.
　　Max. O that thou wert not living, and my Friend. .
　　Æci. I'll bear a wary Eye upon your Actions,
I fear ye *Maximus*, nor can I blame thee
If thou break'ft out, for by the Gods thy Wrong
Deferves a general Ruin: Do ye love me?
　　Max. That's all I have to live on.　　*Æci.* Then go with me,
Ye fhall not to your own Houfe.　　*Max.* Nor to any;
My Griefs are greater far than Walls can compafs,
And yet I wonder how it happens with me,
I am not dangerous, and O' my Confcience
Should I now fee the Emperor i'th' heat on't,
I fhould not chide him for't, an Awe runs through me,
I feel it fenfibly, that binds me to it,
'Tis at my Heart now, there it fits and rules,
And methinks 'tis a pleafure to obey it.
　　Æci. This is a Mafk to cozen me; I know ye,
And how far ye dare do; no *Roman* farther,
Nor with more fearlefs Valour; and I'll watch ye:
Keep that Obedience ftill.　　*Max.* Is a Wife's lofs
(For her abufe, much good may do his Grace,
I'll make as bold with his Wife, if I can)
More than the fading of a few frefh Colours,
More than a lufty Spring loft?
　　Æci. No more, *Maximus*, to one that truly lives.
　　Max. Why then I care not, I can live well enough, *Æcius*.
　　　　　　　　　　　　　　　　　　　　　　　For

For look you, Friend, for Virtue, and those Trifles,
They may be bought, they say.   *Æci.* He's craz'd a little,
His Grief has made him talk things from his Nature.

Max. But Chastity is not a thing, I take it,
To get in *Rome*, unless it be bespoken
A hundred Year before; is it *Æcius?*
By'r Lady, and well handled too i'th' breeding.

Æci. Will ye go any way?   *Max.* I'll tell thee, Friend,
If my Wife for all this should be a Whore now,
A kind of kicker out of Sheets, 'twould vex me,
For I am not angry yet; the Emperor
Is young and handsome, and the Woman Flesh,
And may not these two couple without scratching?

Æci. Alas, my noble Friend.   *Max* Alas not me,
I am not wretched, for there's no Man miserable
But he that makes himself so.   *Æci* Will ye walk yet?

Max. Come, come, she dare not die, Friend, that's the truth on't,
She knows the inticing Sweets and Delicacies
Of a young Prince's pleasures, and I thank her,
She has made a way for *Maximus* to rise by:
Will't not become me bravely? Why do you think
She wept, and said she was Ravish'd? Keep it here
And I'll discover to you   *Æci.* Well.   *Max.* She knows
I love no bitten Flesh, and out of that hope
She might be from me, she contriv'd this Knavery;
Was it not monstrous. Friend?   *Æci.* Does he but seem so,
Or is he Mad indeed?   *Max.* O Gods, my Heart!

Æci. Would it wou'd fairly break.

Max. Methinks I am somewhat wilder than I was,
And yet I thank the Gods I know my Duty.

Enter Claudia

Clau. Nay ye may spare your Tears; she's dead,
She is so.   *Max.* Why so it should be: How?

Clau When first she enter'd
Into her House, after a World of weeping,
And blushing like the Sun-set, as we see her;
Dare I, said she, defile this House with Whore,
In which his noble Family has flourish'd?
At which she fell, and stir'd no more; we rub'd her.

Max. No more of that; be gone.   Now my *Æcius*, [*Exit* Clau
If thou wilt do me pleasure, weep a little,
I am so parch'd I cannot: Your Example
Has brought the Rain down now: Now lead me, Friend,
And as we walk together, let's pray together truly,
I may not fall from Faith.   *Æci.* That's nobly spoken.

                                                          Max.

Max. Was I not wild, *Æcius?*   *Æc.* Somewhat troubled.

Max. I felt no Sorrow then: Now I'll go with ye,
But do not name the Woman: Fye, what Fool
Am I to weep thus? Gods, *Lucina,* take thee,
For thou wert even the best, and worthiest Lady.

Æc. Good Sir, no more, I shall be melted with it.

Max. I have done, and good Sir comfort me.
Would there were Wars now.

Æc. Settle your Thoughts, come.

Max. So I have now, Friend,
Of my deep Lamentations here's an end.   [*Exeunt.*

Enter Pontius, Phidias, *and* Aretus.

Phi. By my Faith, Captain *Pontius,* besides pity
Of your fall'n Fortunes, what to say I know not,
For 'tis too true the Emperor desires not,
But my best Master, any Soldier near him.

Are. And when he understands, he cast your Fortunes
For Disobedience, how can we incline him
(That are but under Persons to his Favours)
To any fair Opinion? Can ye Sing?

Pon. Not to please him, *Aretus,* for my Songs
Go not to th' Lute, or Viol, but to th' Trumpet,
My Tune kept on a Target, and my Subject
The well struck Wounds of Men, not Love, or Women.

Phi. And those he understands not.   *Pon.* He should, *Phidias.*

Are. Could you not leave this killing way a little?
You must if here you would plant your self, and rather
Learn as we do, to like what those affect
That are above us: Wear their Actions,
And think they keep us warm too: What they say,
Though oftentimes they speak a little foolishly,
Not stay to construe, but prepare to execute,
And think however the end falls, the business
Cannot run empty-handed.   *Phi.* Can ye flatter,
And if it were put to you, lie a little?

Pon. Yes, if it be a Living.   *Are.* That's well said then.

Pon. But must these Lies and Flatteries be believ'd, then?

Phi. Oh yes, by any means.   *Pon.* By any means then,
I cannot lie, nor flatter.   *Are.* Ye must swear too,
If ye be there.   *Pon.* I can swear, if they move me.

Phi. Cannot ye forswear too.   *Pon.* The Court for ever,
If it be grown so wicked.

Are. You should procure a little too.   *Pon.* What's that?
Mens honest sayings for my Truth?   *Are.* Oh no, Sir:
But Womens honest Actions for your trial.

Pon. Do you do all these things?   *Phi.* Do you not like 'em?
    Pon.

Pon. Do ye ask me seriously, or trifle with me?
I am not so low yet, to be your Mirth.
　　Are. You do mistake us, Captain, for sincerely,
We ask you how you like 'em?　*Pon.* Then sincerely
I tell ye I abhor 'em: They are ill ways,
And I will starve before I fall into 'em.
The Doers of 'em Wretches, their base hungers
Cares not whose Bread they eat, nor how they get it.
　　Are What then, Sir?　*Pon.* If you profess this Wickedness,
Because ye have been Soldiers, and born Arms,
The Servants of the brave *Æctus,*
And by him put to th' Emperor, give me leave,
Or I must take it else, to say ye are Villains,
For all your Golden Coats, Debosh'd, base Villains,
Yet I do wear a Sword to tell ye so.
Is this the way you mark out for a Soldier,
A Man that has commanded for the Empire,
And born the Reputation of a Man?
Are there not lazy things enough call'd Fools and Cowards,
And poor enough to be preferr'd for Pandars,
But wanting Soldiers must be Knaves too? ha:
This the trim course of Life: Were not ye born Bawds,
And so inherit but your Rights? I am poor,
And may expect a worse; yet digging, pruning,
Mending of broken Ways, carrying of Water,
Planting of Worts, and Onions, any thing
That's honest, and a Man's, I'll rather chuse,
Ay, and live better on it, which is juster,
Drink my well-gotten Water with more Pleasure,
When my Endeavour's done, and Wages paid me,
Than you do Wine, eat my course Bread not curst,
And mend upon't; your Diets are Diseases;
And sleep as soundly, when my Labour bids me,
As any forward Pandar of ye all,
And rise a great deal honester; my Garments,
Though not as yours, the soft sins of the Empire,
Yet may be warm, and keep the biting Wind out,
When every single Breath of poor Opinion
Finds you through all your Velvets.　*Are.* You have hit it,
Nor are we those we seem; the Lord *Æctus*
Put us good Men to th' Emperor, so we have serv'd him,
Though much neglected for it: So dare be still:
Your Curses are not ours: We have seen your Fortune,
But yet know no way to redeem it: Means,
Such as we have, ye shall not want, brave *Pontius,*
But pray be temperate, if we can wipe out

　　　　　　　　　　　　　　　　　　　　　The

The way of your Offences, we are yours, Sir;
And you shall live at Court an honest Man too.
　Phi. That little Meat and Means we have, we'll share it,
Fear not to be as we are; what we told ye,
Were but meer tryals of your Truth : You're worthy,
And so we'll ever hold ye; suffer better,
And then ye are a right Man, *Pontius*;
If my good Master be not ever angry,
Ye shall command again.
　Pon. I have found two good Men: Use my Life,
For it is yours, and all I have to thank ye.　　　　*[Exeunt.*

SCENE III.

Enter Maximus.

　Max There's no way else to do it, he must die,
This Friend must die, this Soul of *Maximus*,
Without whom I am nothing but my Shame,
This perfectness that keeps me from Opinion,
Must dye, or I must live thus branded ever:
A hard choice, and a fatal; Gods ye have given me
A way to credit, but the Ground to go on,
Ye have levell'd with that precious Life I love most.
Yet I must on, and through; for if I offer
To take my way without him, like a Sea
He bears his high Command, 'twixt me and Vengeance,
And in my own Road sinks me, he is honest,
Of a most constant Loyalty to *Cæsar*,
And when he shall but doubt, I dare attempt him,
But make a question of his Ill, but say
What is a *Cæsar*, that he dare do this,
Dead sure he cuts me off: *Æcius* dies,
Or I have lost my self: Why should I kill him?
Why should I kill my self? for 'tis my killing,
Æcius is my Root, and wither him,
Like a decaying Branch, I fall to nothing.
Is he not more to me than Wife, than *Cæsar*?
Though I had now my safe Revenge upon him,
Is he not more than Rumour, and his Friendship
Sweeter than the love of Women? What is Honour
We all so strangely are bewitch'd withal?
Can it relieve me if I want? he has;
Can Honour, 'twixt the incensed Prince, and Envy,
Bear up the Lives of worthy Men? he has;
Can Honour pull the Wings of fearful Cowards,
And make 'em turn again like Tygers? he has,
And I have liv'd to see this, and preserv'd so;

Why

Why should this empty word incite me then
To what is ill, and cruel? let her perish:
A Friend is more than all the World, than Honour;
She is a Woman, and her Loss the-less,
And with her go my Griefs: But hark ye, *Maximus*,
Was she not yours? Did she not die, to tell ye
She was a Ravish'd Woman? Did not Justice
Nobly begin with her, that not deserv'd it,
And shall he live that did it? Stay a little,
Can this Abuse die here? Shall not Mens Tongues
Dispute it afterward, and say I gave
(Affecting dull Obedience, and tame Duty,
And led away with fondness of a Friendship)
The only Virtue of the World to Slander?
Is not this certain, was not she a chaste one,
And such a one, that no compare dwelt with her,
One of so sweet a Virtue, that *Æcius*,
Even he himself, this Friend that holds me from it,
Out of his worthy Love to me, and Justice,
Had it not been on *Cæsar*, he'd reveng'd her?
By Heav'n he told me so; what shall I do then?

Enter a Servant.

Can other Men affect it, and I cole?
I fear he must not live.   *Serv.* My Lord, the General
Is come to seek ye.   *Max.* Go, intreat him to enter:
O brave *Æcius*, I could wish thee now
As far from Friendship to me, as from Fears,
That I might cut thee off, like that I weigh'd not
Is there no way without him, to come near it?
For out of honesty he must destroy me
If I attempt it; he must dye as others,
And I must lose him; 'tis necessity,
Only the time, and means is all the difference;
But yet I would not make a Murther of him,
Take him directly for my doubts; he shall dye,
I have found a way to do it, and a safe one,
It shall be Honour to him too: I know not
What to determine certain, I am so troubled,
And such a deal of Conscience presses me;
Would I were dead my self.

Enter Æcius.

Æci. You run away well;
How got you from me, Friend?
Max. That that leads mad Men;
A strong Imagination made me wander.
Æci. I thought ye had been more settled.   *Max.* I am well,

F   But

But you muſt give me leave a little ſometimes
To have a buzzing in my Brains.   *Æci.* Ye are dangerous,
But I'll prevent it if I can; ye told me
You would go to th' Army.   *Max.* Why, to have my Throat cut,
Muſt he not be the braveſt Man, *Æcius,*
That ſtrikes me firſt ?   *Æci.* You promiſed me a Freedom
From all theſe Thoughts, and why ſhould any ſtrike you ?
   Max I am an Enemy, a wicked one,
Worſe than the Foes of *Rome,* I am a Coward,
A Cuckold, and a Coward, that's two Cauſes
Why every one ſhould beat me.   *Æci.* Ye are neither ;
And durſt another tell me ſo, he dy'd for't.
For thus far on mine Honour, I'll aſſure you
No Man more lov'd than you, and for your Valour,
And what ye may be, fair ; no Man more follow'd
   Max. A doughty Man indeed: But that's all one,
The Emperor, nor all the Princes living
Shall find a flaw in my Coat, I have ſuffer'd,
And can yet ; let them find Inflictions,
I'll find a Body for 'em, or I'll break it.
'Tis not a Wife can thruſt me out; ſome look'd for't,
But let 'em look 'till they are blind with looking,
They are but Fools, yet there is Anger in me,
That I would fain diſperſe, and now I think on't,
You told me, Friend, the Provinces are ſtirring,
We ſhall have ſport I hope then, and what's dangerous
A Battel ſhall beat from me.   *Æci* Why do ye eye me
With ſuch a ſettled look?   *Max.* Pray tell me this,
Do we not love extremely? I love you ſo.
   Æci. If I ſhould ſay I lov'd not you as truly,
I ſhould do that I never durſt do, lie.
   Max If I ſhould dye, would it not grieve you much?
   Æci. Without all doubt.   *Max.* And could you live without me?
   Æci. It would much trouble me to live without ye,
Our Loves, and loving Souls have been ſo us'd
But to one Houſhold in us: But to dye
Becauſe I could not make you live, were Woman,
Far much too weak, were it to ſave your Worth,
Or to redeem your Name from rooting out,
To quit you bravely fighting from the Foe,
Or fetch ye off, where Honour had ingag'd ye,
I ought, and would dye for ye. *Max.* Truly ſpoken.
What Beaſt but I, that muſt, could hurt this Man now ?
Would he had raviſh'd me, I would have paid him,
I would have taught him ſuch a Trick, his Eunuchs
Nor all his black-ey'd Boys dreamt of yet ;

                                                      By

By all the Gods I am mad now; now were *Cæfar*
Within my reach, and on his glorious top
The Pile of all the World, he went to nothing;
The Deftinies, nor all the Dames of Hell,
Were I once grapl'd with him, fhould relieve him,
No not the hope of Mankind more; all perifhed;
But this is Words and Weaknefs.

   Æci. Ye look ftrangely.

   Max. I look but as I am, I am a Stranger.

   Æci. To me?

   Max. To every one, I am no *Roman*;
Nor what I am do I know.

   Æci. Then I'll leave ye.

   Max I find I am beft fo, if ye meet with *Maximus*
Pray bid him be an honeft Man for my fake,
You may do much upon him; for his Shadow,
Let me alone.

   Æci. Ye were not wont to talk thus,
And to your Friend; ye have fome Danger in you,
That willingly would run to Action.
Take heed, by all our love take heed.

   Max I, Danger?
I, willing to do any thing, I dig.
Has not my Wife been dead two Days already?
Are not my Mournings by this time Moth-eaten?
Are not her Sins difpers'd to other Women,
And many one ravifh'd to relieve her?
Have I fhed Tears thefe twelve Hours?

   Æci. Now ye weep.

   Max. Some lazy drops that ftaid behind.

   Æci. I'll tell ye,
And I muft tell ye Truth, were it not hazard,
And almoft certain Lofs of all the Empire,
I would win with ye: Were it any Man's
But his Life, that is Life of us, he loft it
For doing of this Mifchief: I would take it,
And to your reft give ye a brave Revenge :
But as the Rule now ftands, and as he rules,
And as the Nations hold in Difobedience,
One Pillar failing, all muft fall; I dare not:
Nor is it juft you fhould be fuffer'd in it,
Therefore again take heed : On foreign Foes
We are our own Revengers, but at Home
On Princes that are eminent and ours,
'Tis fit the Gods fhould judge us : Be not rafh,
Nor let your angry Steel cut thofe ye know not;

For

For by this fatal Blow, if ye dare ftrike it,
As I fee great Aims in ye, thofe unborn yet,
And thofe to come, of them and thefe fucceeding,
Shall bleed the Wrath of *Maximus*: For me,
As ye now bear your felf, I am your Friend ftill,
If ye fall off I will not flatter ye;
And in my Hands, were ye my Soul, you perifh'd:
Once more be careful, ftand, and ftill be worthy,
I'll leave ye for this Hour.   [*Exit.*

   Max. Pray do. 'Tis done:
And Friendfhip, fince thou canft not hold in Dangers,
Give me a certain Ruin, I muft through it.   [*Exit.*

ACT IV. SCENE I.

Enter Emperor, Lycinius, Chilax, *and* Balbus.

Emp. DEAD?   *Chi.* So 'tis thought, Sir.
   Emp. How?   *Lyc.* Grief, and Difgrace,
As People fay.   *Emp.* No more, I have too much on't,
Too much by you, you whetters of my Follies,
Ye Angel formers of my Sins, but Devils;
Where is your cunning now? You would work Wonders,
There was no Chaftity above your Practice,
You would undertake to make her love her Wrongc,
And doat upon her Rape: Mark what I tell ye,
If fhe be dead—— *Chi* Alas, Sir! *Emp.* Hang ye Rafcals,
Ye blafters of my Youth, if fhe be gone,
'Twere better ye had been your Fathers Camels,
Ground under daily weights of Wood and Water:
Am I not *Cæfar*?   *Lyc.* Mighty, and our Maker.
   Emp. Than thus have given my Pleafures to Deftruction.
Look fhe be living, Slaves.   *Lyc* We are no Gods, Sir,
If fhe be dead, to make her new again.
   Emp She cannot dye, fhe muft not dye; are thofe
I plant my Love upon but common Livers?
Their Hours as others, told 'em? Can they be Afhes?
Why do ye flatter a Belief into me
That I am all that is, the World's my Creature,
The Trees bring forth their Fruits when I fay Summer,
The Wind, that knows no limit but his wildnefs,
At my Command moves not a Leaf; the Sea
With his proud Mountain Waters envying Heav'n,
When I fay Still, run into chriftal Mirrors,
Can I do this and fhe dye? Why ye Bubbles,
That with my leaft Breath break, no more remember'd;

                                          Ye

Ye Moths that fly about my Flame and perish,
Ye golden Canker-worms, that eat my Honours,
Living no longer than my Spring of Favour:
Why do ye make me God that can do nothing?
Is she not dead?   *Chi.* All Women are not with her.
    Emp. A common Whore serves you, and far above ye,
The Pleasures of a Body lam'd with Lewdness;
A meer perpetual Motion makes ye happy:
Am I a Man to traffick with Diseases?
Can any but a Chastity serve *Cæsar?*
And such a one the Gods would kneel to purchase?
You think, because you have bred me up to Pleasures,
And almost run me over all the rare ones,
Your Wives will serve the turn: I care not for 'em.
Your Wives are Fencers Whores, and shall be Footmens.
Though sometimes my nice Will, or rather Anger
Have made ye Cuckolds for variety;
I would not have ye hope, nor dream, ye poor ones,
Always so great a Blessing from me; go
Get your own Infamy hereafter, Rascals,
I have done too nobly for ye, ye enjoy
Each one an Heir, the royal Seed of *Cæsar,*
And I may curse ye for't; your wanton Gennets,
That are so Proud, the Wind gets 'em with Fillies,
Taught me this foul Intemperance. Thou *Licinius,*
Hast such a *Messalina,* such a *Lais,*
The Backs of Bulls cannot content, nor Stallions,
The Sweat of fifty Men a Night do's nothing
    Lic. Your Grace but jests, I hope.   *Emp.* 'Tis Oracle.
The Sins of other Women put by hers
Shew off like Sanctities: Thine's a Fool, *Chilax,*
Yet she can tell to twenty, and all Lovers,
And all lien with her too, and all as she is,
Rotten, and ready for an Hospital.
Yours is a holy Whore, Friend *Balbus.*   *Bal* Well, Sir
    Emp One that can pray away the Sins she suffers,
But not the Punishments: She has had ten Bastards,
Five of 'em now are Lictors, yet she prays;
She has been the Song of *Rome,* and common *Pasquil;*
Since I durst see a Wench, she was Camp Mistress,
And muster'd all the Cohorts, paid 'em too,
They have it yet to shew, and yet she prays;
She is now to enter old Men that are Children,
And have forgot their Rudiments: Am I
Left for these wither'd Vices? And but one,
But one of all the World that could content me,

                                        And

And fnatch'd away in fhewing? If your Wives
Be not yet Witches, or your felves, now be fo
And fave your Lives, raife me this noble Beauty
As when I forc'd her, full of Conftancy,
Or by the Gods——　*Lic.* Moft facred *Cæfar.*　*Emp.* Slaves.
　Lic. Good *Proculus.*　*Pro.* By Heav'n you fhall not fee it,
It may concern the Empire.　*Emp.* Ha! What faid'ft thou?
Is fhe not dead?　*Pro.* Not any one I know, Sir;
I come to bring your Grace a Letter, here
Scatter'd belike i'th' Court: 'Tis fent to *Maximus*,
And bearing Danger in it.　*Emp.* Danger? Where?
Double our Guard.　*Pro.* Nay no where, but i'th' Letter.
　Emp. What an afflicted Confcience do I live with,
And what a Beaft am I grown? I had forgotten
To ask Heav'n Mercy for my Fault, and was now
Even ravifh'ng again her Memory.
I find there muft be Danger in this Deed ·
Why do I ftand difputing then, and whining?
For what is not the Gods to give, they cannot,
Though they would link their Powers in one, do mifchief.
This Letter may betray me; get ye gone;
And wait me in the Garden, guard the Houfe well,　　　[*Exeunt.*
And keep this from the Emprefs. The Name *Maximus*
Runs through me like a Feaver; this may be
Some private Letter upon private Bufinefs,
Nothing concerning me: Why fhould I open't?
I have done him wrong enough already; yet
It may concern me too, the Time fo tells me;
The wicked Deed I have done, affures me 'tis fo.
Be what it will, I'll fee it, if that be not
Part of my Fears, among my other Sins,
I'll purge it out in Prayers How? What's this?
Letter read] Lord *Maximus*, you love *Æcius*,
And are his noble Friend too; bid him be lefs,
I mean lefs with the People, Times are dangerous:
The Army is his; the Emperor in doubts,
And as fome will not ftick to fay, declining;
You ftand a conftant Man in either Fortunes;
Perfwade him, he is loft elfe: Though Ambition
Be the laft Sin he touches at, or never;
Yet what the People mad with loving him,
And as they willingly defire another,
May tempt him to, or rather force his Goodnefs,
Is to be doubted mainly: He is all,
(As he ftands now) but the meer name of *Cæfar*;
And fhould the Emperor inforce him leffer,

Not coming from himself, it were more dangerous:
He is Honest, and will hear you: Doubts are scatter'd,
And almost come to growth in every Houshold:
Yet in my foolish Judgment, were this master'd;
The People that are now but Rage, and his,
Might be again Obedience: You shall know me
When *Rome* is fair again; 'till when I love you.
No Name! This may be cunning, yet it seems not;
For there is nothing in it but is certain,
Besides my safety.   Had not good *Germanicus*,
That was as Loyal, and as straight as he is,
If not prevented by *Tiberius*,
Been by the Soldiers forc'd their Emperor?
He had, and 'tis my Wisdom to remember it.
And was not *Corbulo,* even that *Corbulo,*
That ever Fortunate and living *Roman,*
That broke the Heart Strings of the *Parthians,*
And brought *Arsases* Line upon their Knees,
Chain'd to the Awe of *Rome,* because he was thought
(And but in Wine once) fit to make a *Cæsar,*
Cut off by *Nero?* I must seek my Safety:
For 'tis the same again, if not beyond it:
I know the Soldier loves him more than Heav'n,
And will adventure all his Gods to raise him;
Me he hates more than Peace: What this may breed,
If dull Security and Confidence
Let him grow up, a Fool may find, and laugh at.
But why Lord *Maximus,* I injur'd so,
Should be the Man to counsel him, I know not;
More than he has been Friend, and lov'd Allegiance.
What now he is I fear, for his Abuses
Without the People dare draw Blood.   Who waits there?
Enter a Servant.

Serv. Your Grace.   *Emp.* Call *Phidias* and *Aretus* hither:
I'll find a Day for him too; times are dangerous,
The Army his, the Emperor in Doubts:
I find it is too true; did he not tell me,
As if he had intent to make me Odious,
And to my Face, and by a way of Terror,
What Vices I was grounded in, and almost
Proclaim'd the Soldiers hate against me? Is not
The sacred Name and Dignity of *Cæsar*
(Were this *Æcius* more than Man) sufficient
To shake off all his Honesty? He's dangerous
Though he be good, and though a Friend, a fear'd one,
And such I must not sleep by: Are they come yet?

H

I do believe this Fellow, and I thank him;
'Twas time to look about, if I muſt periſh,
Yet ſhall my Fears go foremoſt.

Enter Phidias *and* Aretus.

Phi. Life to *Cæſar*.

Emp. Is Lord *Æcius* waiting? *Phi.* Not this Morning,
I rather think he's with the Army. *Emp.* Army?
I do not like that Army: Go unto him,
And bid him ſtraight attend me, and do ye hear,
Come private without any; I have Buſineſs
Only for him. *Phi.* Your Grace's Pleaſure. [*Exit* Phidias.

Emp. Go;
What Soldier is the ſame, I have ſeen him often,
That keeps you Company, *Aretus?* *Are.* Me, Sir?

Emp. Ay, you Sir.

Are. One they call *Pontius*, an't pleaſe your Grace.

Emp. A Captain? *Are.* Yes, he was ſo;
But ſpeaking ſomething roughly in his Want,
Eſpecially of Wars, the noble General
Out of a ſtrict Allegiance caſt his Fortunes.

Emp. H'as been a valiant Fellow. *Are* So he's ſtill.

Emp. Alas, the General might have pardon'd Follies,
Soldiers will Talk ſometimes. *Are.* I am glad of this.

Emp He wants Preferment, as I take it. *Are.* Yes, Sir;
And for that noble Grace his Life ſhall ſerve.

Emp. I have a Service for him:
I ſhame a Soldier ſhould become a Beggar;
I like the Man, *Aretus* *Are* Gods protect ye.

Emp. Bid him repair to *Proculus*, and there
He ſhall receive the Buſineſs, and Reward for't:
I'll ſee him ſetled too, and as a Soldier,
We ſhall want ſuch.
The Sweets of Heav'n ſtill Crown ye,
I have a fearful Darkneſs in my Soul,
And 'till I be deliver'd, ſtill am dying. [*Exeunt.*

SCENE II.

Enter Maximus *alone.*

Max. My way has taken: All the Court's in Guard,
And Buſineſs every where, and every Corner
Full of ſtrange Whiſpers: I am leaſt in Rumour,

Enter Æcius *and* Phidias.

And ſo I'll keep my ſelf. Here comes *Æcius,*
I ſee the Bait is ſwallow'd: If he be loſt
He is my Martyr, and my way ſtands open,
And Honour on thy Head, his Blood is reckon'd. *Æci.*

Æci. Why how now Friend, what make ye here unarm'd?
Are ye turn'd Merchant? *Max.* By your fair perſwaſion,
And ſuch a Merchant trafficks without danger;
I have forgotten all, *Æctius,*
And which is more, forgiven. *Æci.* Now I love ye,
Truly I do, ye are a worthy *Roman.*

Max. The fair Repentance of my Prince to me
Is more than Sacrifice of Blood and Vengeance;
No Eyes ſhall weep her Ruins, but mine own.

Æci. Still ye take more Love from me: Virtuous Friend,
The Gods make poor *Æcius* worthy of thee.

Max. Only in me y'are poor, Sir · And I worthy
Only in being yours: But why your Arm thus,
Have ye been hurt, *Æcius?* *Æci.* Bruis'd a little;
My Horſe fell with me, Friend; which 'till this Morning
I never knew him do. *Max.* Pray Gods it bode well;
And now I think on't better, ye ſhall back,
Let my Perſwaſions rule ye. *Æci.* Back! Why, *Maximus?*
The Emperor commands me come. *Max.* I like not
At this time his Command. *Æci.* I do at all Times,
And all Times will obey it, why not now then?

Max. I'll tell ye why, and as I have been govern'd,
Be you ſo, noble Friend: The Court's in Guard,
Arm'd ſtrongly, for what Purpoſe, let me fear;
I do not like your going. *Æci.* Were it Fire,
And that Fire certain to conſume this Body,
If *Cæſar* ſent, I would go; never fear, Man,
If he take me, he takes his Arms away.
I am too plain and true to be ſuſpected.

Max. Then I have dealt unwiſely. *Æci.* If the Emperor,
Becauſe he meerly may, will have my Life,
That's all he has to work on, and all ſhall have:
Let him, he loves me better: Here I wither,
And happily may live, 'till ignorantly
I run into a Fault worth Death: Nay more, Diſhonour.
Now all my Sins, I dare ſay thoſe of Duty
Are printed here, and if I fall ſo happy,
I bleſs the Grave I lye in, and the Gods
Equal, as dying on the Enemy,
Muſt take me up a Sacrifice. *Max.* Go on then,
And I'll go with ye. *Æci.* No, ye may not, Friend.

Max. He cannot be a Friend, bars me *Æcius;*
Shall I forſake ye in my doubts? *Æci.* Ye muſt.

Max. I muſt not, nor I will not; have I liv'd
Only to be a Carpet Friend for pleaſure?
I can endure a Death as well as *Cato*

G

Æci.

Nor none muſt go along.   *Max.* I have a Sword too,
And once I could have us'd it for my Friend.
    Æci. I need no Sword, nor Friend in this, pray leave me;
And as ye love me, do not over-love me;
I am commanded none ſhall come: At Supper
I'll meet ye, and we'll drink a Cup or two;
Ye need good Wine, ye have been ſad : Farewel.
    Max. Farewel my noble Friend, let me embrace ye
E'er ye depart; it may be one of us
Shall never do the like again.   *Æci.* Yes often.
    Max. Farewel, good dear *Æcius.*   *Æci.* Farewel *Maximus,*
'Till Night: Indeed you doubt too much.   [*Exit.*
    Max. I do not:
Go worthy Innocent, and make the number
Of *Cæſar*'s ſins ſo great, Heav'n may want Mercy.
I'll hover hereabout to know what paſſes:
And if he be ſo deviliſh to deſtroy thee,
In thy Blood ſhall begin his Tragedy.

                                    [*Exit.*

S C E N E III.

Enter Proculus, *and* Pontius.

    Pro. Beſides this, if you do it, you enjoy
The noble Name *Patrician* : More than that too,
The Friend of *Cæſar* ye are ſtil'd: there's nothing
Within the hopes of *Rome*, or preſent being,
But you may ſafely ſay is yours.   *Pon.* Pray ſtay, Sir;
What has *Æcius* done to be deſtroy'd?
At leaſt I would have a colour.   *Pro.* Ye have more,
Nay all that may be given, he is a Traitor,
One, any Man would ſtrike that were a Subject.
    Pon. Is he ſo foul ?   *Pro.* Yes a moſt fearful Traitor.
    Pon. A fearful Plague upon thee, for thou lyeſt.
I ever thought the Soldier would undo him
With his too much Affection.   *Pro.* Ye have hit it,
They have brought him to Ambition.
    Pon. Then he is gone.
    Pro. The Emperor, out of a fooliſh pity,
Would ſave him yet.   *Pon.* Is he ſo mad?   *Pro.* He's madder
Would go to th' Army to him.   *Pon.* Would 'a ſo?
    Pro. Yes, *Pontius*; but we conſider——   *Pon.* Wiſely.
    Pro. How elſe, Man, that the State lies in it.
    Pon. And your Lives too.   *Pro.* And every Man's.   *Pon.* He did me
All the Diſgrace he could.   *Pro.* And ſcurvily.
    Pon. Out of a Miſchief meerly: Did you mark it?
    Pro. Yes, well enough. Now ye have means to quit it;

                                                    The

The deed done, take his Place.　　*Pon.* Pray let me think on't,
'Tis ten to one I do it.　　*Pro.* Do, and be happy.　　[*Exit* Pro.

　　Pon. This Emperor is made of nought but mischief,
Sure, Murther was his Mother: None to lop,
But the main Link he had? Upon my Conscience
The Man is truly honest, and that kills him,
For to live here, and study to be true,
Is all one to be Traitors: Why should he dye?
Have they not Slaves and Rascals for their Off'rings
In full abundance; Bawds more than Beasts for slaughter
Have they not singing Whores enough, and Knaves too,
And millions of such Martyrs to sink *Charon*,
But the best Sons of *Rome* must sail too? I will shew him
(Since he must Dye) a way to do it truly:
And though he bears me hard, yet shall he know,
I am born to make him bless me for a Blow.　　　　[*Exit.*

SCENE IV.

Enter Phidias, Aretus *and* Æcius:

　　Pbi. Yet ye may 'scape to th' Camp, we'll hazard with ye.
　　Are. Lose not your Life so basely, Sir: Ye are arm'd,
And many when they see your Sword out, and know why,
Must follow your Adventure.　　*Æci.* Get ye from me;
Is not the Doom of *Cæsar* on this Body,
Do not I bear my last Hour here, now sent me?
Am I not old *Æcius*, ever dying?
You think this Tenderness and Love you bring me,
'Tis Treason, and the strength of Disobedience,
And if ye tempt me further, ye shall feel it:
I seek the Camp for Safety, when my Death
Ten times more glorious than my Life, and lasting
Bids me be happy: Let the Fool fear dying,
Or he that weds a Woman for his Honour,
Dreaming no other Life to come but Kisses;
Æcius is not now to learn to suffer:
If ye dare shew a just Affection, kill me,
I stay but those that must: Why do ye weep?
Am I so wretched to deserve Mens Pities?
Go give your Tears to those that lose their Worths,
Bewail their Miseries, for me wear Garlands,
Drink Wine, and much; sing Peans to my Praise,
I am to triumph, Friends, and more than *Cæsar*,
For *Cæsar* fears to die, I love to die.
　　Pbi. O my dear Lord!　　*Æci.* No more, go, go, I say;
Shew me not signs of Sorrow, I deserve none;
Dare any Man lament, I should die nobly?
　　　　　　　G 2　　　　　　　　　　　　　　　Are

Am I grown Old to have such Enemies?
When I am dead, speak honourably of me,
That is, preserve my Memory from dying;
There if you needs must weep your ruin'd Master,
A Tear or two will seem well: This I charge ye,
(Because ye say you yet love old *Æcius*)
See my poor Body burnt, and some to sing
About my Pile, and what I have done and suffer'd,
If *Cæsar* kill not that too: At your Banquets,
When I am gone, if any chance to number
The Times that have been sad and dangerous,
Say how I fell, and 'tis sufficient:
No more I say, he that laments my End
By all the Gods dishonours me; begone
And suddenly, and wisely from my Dangers,
My Death is catching else.   *Phi.* We fear not dying.
  Æci. Yet fear a wilful Death, the just Gods hate it,
I need no Company to that, that Children
Dare do alone, and Slaves are proud to purchase;
Live 'till your Honesties, as mine has done,
Make this corrupted Age sick of your Virtues,
Then die a Sacrifice, and then ye know
The noble Use of dying well, and *Roman*.
  Are. And must we leave ye, Sir?   *Æci.* We must all die,
All leave our selves, it matters not, where, when,
Nor how, so we die well: And can that Man that does so
Need Lamentation for him? Children weep
Pecause they have offended, or for Fear,
Women for want of Will, and Anger; is there
In noble Man, that truly feels both poises
Of Life and Death, so much of this wet weakness
To drown a glorious Death in Child and Woman?
I am asham'd to see ye; yet ye move me,
And were it not my Manhood would accuse me,
For covetous to live, I should weep with ye.
  Phi. O we shall never see you more.   *Æci.* 'Tis true;
Nor I the miseries that *Rome* shall suffer,
Which is a benefit Life cannot reckon:
But what I have been, which is just and faithful;
One that grew old for *Rome,* when *Rome* forgot him,
And for he was an honest Man durst die,
Ye shall have daily with ye: Could that dye too,
And I return no Traffick of my Travels,
No pay to have been Soldier, but this Silver,
No *Annals* of *Æcius,* but he liv'd,
My Friends ye had cause to weep, and bitterly;

The

The common Overflows of tender Women,
And Children new born crying, were too little
To shew me then most wretched: If Tears must be,
I should in Justice weep 'em, and for you,
You are to live, and yet behold those slaughters
The dry and wither'd Bones of Death would bleed at:
But sooner, than I have time to think what must be,
I fear you'll find what shall be; if ye love me,
Let that word serve for all; be gone and leave me;
I have some little practice with my Soul,
And then the sharpest Sword is welcom'st; go,
Pray be gone, ye have obey'd me living,
Be not for shame now stubborn; so I thank ye,
And farewel, a better Fortune guide ye. [*Ex.* Phi. *and* Are.
I am a little thirsty, not for fear,
And yet it is a kind of fear, I say so;
Is it to be a just Man now again,
And leave my Flesh unthought of? 'Tis departed:
I hear 'em come, who strikes first?
I stay for ye:

Enter Balbus, Chilax *and* Lycinius.

Yet I will dye a Soldier, my Sword drawn,
But against none: Why do ye fear? Come forward.
  Bal. You were a Soldier, *Chilax. Chi.* Yes, I muster'd,
But never saw the Enemy. *Lyc.* He's drawn,
By Heav'n I dare not do it. *Æci.* Why do ye tremble?
I am to die, come ye not now from *Cæsar,*
To that end, speak? *Bal.* We do, and we must kill ye,
'Tis *Cæsar's* will. *Chi.* I charge you put your Sword up,
That we may do it handsomely. *Æci.* Ha, ha, ha,
My Sword up, handsomly? where were ye bred?
Ye are the merriest Murderers, my Masters,
I ever met withal; come forward Fools,
Why do ye stare? Upon mine Honour, Bawds,
I will not strike ye. *Lyc.* I'll not be first. *Bal.* Nor I.
  Chi. You had best die quietly · The Emperor
Sees how you bear your self. *Æci.* I would die, Rascals,
If you would kill me quietly. *Bal.* ———— Of *Proculus,*
He promis'd us to bring a Captain hither,
That has been us'd to kill. *Æci.* I'll call the Guard,
Unless you will kill me quickly, and proclaim
What beastly, base, and cowardly Companions,
The Emperor has trusted with his safety:
Nay I'll give out, ye fell of my side, Villains.
Strike home, ye bawdy Slaves. *Chi.* By Heav'n he'll kill us,
I mark'd his Hand, he waits but time to reach us,

Now

Now do you offer.   *Æct.* If ye do mangle me,
And kill me not at two Blows, or at three,
Or not so stagge me, my Senses fail me,
Look to your selves.
    Chi. I told ye.   *Æct.* Strike me manly,
And take a thousand Strokes.
            Enter Pontius.
    Bal. Here's *Pontius.*
    Pon. Not kill'd him yet?
Is this the Love ye bear the Emperor?
Nay then, I see ye are Traitors all, have at ye.   [*Lyc runs away.*
    Chi. Oh I am hurt! *Bal.* And I am kill'd.   [*Ex. Chi and* Bal.
    Pon. Die Bawds,
As ye have liv'd and flourish'd.   *Æci.* Wretched Fellow,
What hast thou done?   *Pon.* Kill'd them that durst not kill,
And you are next.   *Æci.* Art thou not *Pontius?*
    Pon. I am the same you cast, *Æcius,*
And in the Face of all the Camp disgrac'd.
    Æci. Then so much nobler, as thou wert a Soldier,
Shall my Death be: Is it Revenge provok'd thee,
Or art thou hir'd to kill me? *Pon.* Both. *Æct.* Then do it.
    Pon. Is that all? *Æci.* Yes. *Pon.* Would you not live?
    Æci. Why should I,
To thank thee for my Life?   *Pon.* Yes, if I spare it.
    Æci. Be not deceiv'd, I was not made to thank
For any Courtesie, but killing me,
A Fellow of thy Fortune; do thy Duty.
    Pon. Do not you fear me? *Æci.* No *Pon.* Nor love me for it?
    Æci. That's as thou dost thy Business. *Pon.* When you are dead,
Your Place is mine, *Æcius.*   *Æci.* Now I fear thee,
And not alone thee *Pontius,* but the Empire.
    Pon. Why, I can govern, Sir   *Æci.* I would thou could'st
And first thy self: Thou canst fight well, and bravely,
Thou canst endure all Dangers, Heats, Colds, Hungers;
Heav'ns angry Flashes are not suddener,
Than I have seen thee execute; nor more mortal;
The winged Feet of flying Enemies
I have stood and view'd thee Mow away like Rushes,
And still kill the Killer: Were thy Mind
But half so sweet in Peace, as rough in Dangers,
I dy'd to leave a happy Heir behind me;
Come strike, and be a General.   *Pon.* Prepare then:
And for I see your Honour cannot lessen,
And 'twere a shame for me to strike a dead Man,
Fight your short Span out.   *Æci.* No, thou know'st I must not,
I dare not give thee so much 'Vantage of me,

                            As

As Difobedience.   *Pon.* Dare ye not defend ye,
Againft your Enemy?   *Æct.* Not fent from *Cæfar,*
I have no Power to make fuch Enemies;
For as I am condemn'd, my naked Sword
Stands but a Hatchment by me; only held
To fhew I was a Soldier.   Had not *Cæfar*
Chain'd all Defence in this Doom, Let him die,
Old as I am, and quench'd with Scars, and Sorrows,
Yet would I make this wither'd Arm do wonders,
And open in an Enemy fuch Wounds
Mercy would weep to look on.   *Pon.* Then have at ye,
And look upon me, and be fure ye fear not.
Remember who you are, and why you live,
And what I have been to you. Cry not hold,
Nor think it bafe Injuftice I fhould kill ye.
   Æct. I am prepar'd for all.   *Pon.* For now, *Æctus,*
Thou fhalt behold and find I was no Traitor,
And as I do it, blefs me; die as I do.   [*Pon kills himfelf.*
   Æci Thou haft deceiv'd me, *Pontius,* and I thank thee;
By all my hopes in Heav'n, thou art a *Roman.*
   Pon. To fhew you what you ought to do, this is not;
For flander's felf would fhame to find you Coward,
Or willing to out-live your Honefty:
But noble Sir, ye have been jealous of me,
And held me in the Rank of dangerous Perfons,
And I muft dying fay it was but Juftice,
Ye caft me from my Credit; yet believe me,
For there is nothing now but Truth to fave me,
And your Forgivenefs, though ye held me hainous,
And of a troubled Spirit, that like Fire
Turns all to Flames it meets with, ye miftook me;
If I were Foe to any thing, 'twas Eafe,
Want of the Soldiers Due, the Enemy,
The Nakednefs we found at home, and Scorn,
Children of Peace, and Pleafures, no regard
Nor comfort for our Scars, but how we got 'em,
To rufty Time, that eat our Bodies up,
And even began to prey upon our Honours,
To wants at Home, and more than Wants, Abufes;
To them, that when the Enemy invaded
Made us their Saints, but now the Sores of *Rome;*
To filken Flattery, and Pride plain'd over,
Forgetting with what Wind then Feathers fail,
And under whofe Protection their foft Pleafures
Grow full and numberlefs: To this I am Foe,
Not to the State, or any point of Duty:

                                And

And let me speak but what a Soldier may,
Truly I ought to be so; yet I err'd,
Because a far more noble Sufferer
Shew'd me the way to patience, and I lost it:
This is the end I die, Sir; to live basely,
And not the Follower of him that bred me,
In full account and Virtue, *Pontius* dare not,
Much less to out-live what is good, and flatter.

Æct. I want a Name to give thy Virtue, Soldier,
For only Good is far below thee, *Pontius,*
The Gods shall find thee one; thou hast fashion'd Death,
In such an Excellent and Beauteous manner,
I wonder Men can live: Canst thou speak once more,
For thy Words are such Harmony, a Soul
Would chuse to fly to Heav'n in. *Pon.* A farewel:
Good noble General your Hand, forgive me,
And think what ever was displeasing you,
Was none of mine: Ye cannot live. *Æci.* I will not:
Yet one word more. *Pon.* Dye nobly: *Rome* farewel:
And *Valentinian* fall, thou hast broke thy bases.
In Joy ye have given me a quiet Death,
I would strike more Wounds, if I had more Breath. [*Dies.*

Æct. Is there an hour of Goodness beyond this?
Or any Man would out-live such a dying,
Would *Cæsar* double all my Honours on me,
And stick me o'er with Favours, like a Mistress;
Yet would I grow to this Man: I have lov'd,
But never doated on a Face 'till now:
O Death thou art more than Beauty, and thy pleasure
Beyond Posterity: Come Friends and kill me;
Cæsar be kind, and send a thousand Swords,
The more, the greater is my fall: Why stay ye?
Come, and I'll kiss your Weapons: Fear me not,
By all the Gods I'll honour ye for killing:
Appear, or through the Court, and World, I'll search ye:
My Sword is gone; Ye are Traitors if ye spare me,
And *Cæsar* must consume ye; all base Cowards?
I'll follow ye, and e'er I dye proclaim ye,
The Weeds of *Italy*; the Dross of Nature.
Where are ye, Villains, Traitors, Slaves. [*Exit.*

Enter Proculus, *and three others running over the Stage.*

Pro. I knew h'ad kill'd the Captain. 1. Here's his Sword.

Pro. Let it alone, 'twill fight it self else; Friends,
An hundred Men are not enough to do it,
I'll to the Emperor and get more Aid.

Æct. None strike a poor condemn'd Man! *Pro.* He is Mad:
Shift

Shift for your felves, my Mafters.   [*Exeunt·*
Enter Æcius.

Æci. Then *Æcius,*
See what thou dar'ft thy felf; hold my good Sword,
Thou haft been kept from Blood too long, I'll kifs thee,
For thou art more than Friend now, my Preferver,
Shew me the way to Happinefs, I feek it:
And all you great ones, that have fall'n as I do,
To keep your Memories and Honours living,
Be prefent in your Virtues, and affift me,
That like ftrong *Cato,* I may put away
All Promifes, but what fhall crown my Afhes;
Rome, Fare thee well. Stand long, and know to Conquer
Whilft there is People, and Ambition :
Now for a Stroke fhall turn me to a Star:
I come ye bleffed Spirits, make me Room
To live for ever in *Elizium:*
Do Men fear this? O that Pofterity
Could learn from him but this, that loves his Wound,
There is no Pain at all in dying well,
Nor none are loft, but thofe that make their Hell. [*Kills himfelf.*
                    Enter Proculus *and two others.*

1 *Within.* He's dead, draw in the Guard again.
    Pro. He's dead indeed,
And I am glad he's gone; he was a Devil:
His Body, if his Eunuchs come, is theirs;
The Emperor, out of his Love to Virtue,
Has given 'em that: Let no Man ftop their Entrance   [*Exit.*
                    Enter Phidias *and* Aretus.

    Phi. O my moft noble Lord! Look here *Aretus,*
Here's a fad fight.   *Are.* O Cruelty! O *Cæfar!*
O Times that bring forth nothing but Deftruction,
And Overflows of Blood ! Why waft thou kill'd
Is it to be a juft Man now again,
As when *Tiberius* and wild *Nero* reign'd,
Only affurance of his Overthrow ?
    Phi. It is, *Aretus*: He that would live now,
Muft, like the Toad, feed only on Corruptions,
And grow with thofe to Greatnefs: Honeft Virtue,
And the true *Roman* Honour, Faith and Valour,
That have been all the Riches of the Empire,
Now like the fearful Tokens of the Plague,
Are meer fore-runners of their ends that owe 'em.
    Are. Never enough lamented Lord : Dear Mafter,
                    Enter Maximus.
Of whom now fhall we learn to live like Men?

                    H

                                        From

From **whom** draw out our Actions juft and worthy?
Oh thou art **gone**, and gone with thée all Goodnefs,
The great Example of all Equity,
O thou alone a *Roman*, thou art perifh'd,
Faith, Fortitude, and conftant Noblenefs;
Weep *Rome*, weep *Italy*, weep all that knew him,
And you that fear'd him as a noble Foe,
(If Enemies have honourable Tears)
Weep this decay'd *Æcius* fall'n, and fcatter'd————
By foul and bafe Suggeftion.   *Phi.* O Lord *Maximus*,
This was your worthy Friend.   *Max.* The Gods forgive me:
Think not the worfe, my Friends, I fhed not Tears,
Great Griefs lament within; yet now I have found 'em:
Would I had never known the World, nor Women,
Nor what that curfed Name of Honour was,
So this were once again *Æcius*:
But I am deftin'd to a mighty Action,
And beg my pardon, Friend, my Vengeance taken,
I will not be long from thee : Ye have a great lofs,
But bear it patiently, yet to fay Truth,
In Juftice 'tis not fufferable: I am next,
And were it now, I would be glad on't: Friends,
Who fhall preferve you now?   *Are.* Nay, we are loft too.
    Max. I fear ye are, for likely fuch as love
The Man that's fall'n, and have been nourifh'd by him,
Do not ftay long behind: 'Tis held no Wifdom.
I know what I muft do, O my *Æcius*,
Canft thou thus perifh, pluck'd up by the Roots,
And no Man feel thy Worthinefs? From Boys
He bred you both, I think.   *Phi* And from the pooreft.
    Max. And lov'd ye as his own.   *Are.* We found it, Sir.
    Max Is not this a lofs then?   *Phi.* O, a lofs of loffes;
Our Lives, and ruins of our Families,
The utter being nothing of our Names,
Were nothing near it.   *Max.* As I take it too,
He put ye to the Emperor.   *Are* He did fo.
    Max. And kept ye ftill in Credit.   *Phi.* 'Tis moft true, Sir.
    Max He fed your Fathers too, and made them Means,
Your fifters he prefer'd to noble Wedlocks,
Did he not, Friends?   *Are* O yes, Sir.   *Max.* As I take it
This worthy Man would not be now forgotten,
I tell ye to my Grief, he was bafely murder'd;
And fomething would be done, by thofe that lov'd him:
And fomething may be: Pray ftand off a little.
Let me bewail him private: O my deareft.
    Phi. Aretus, if we be not fudden, he out-does us,
I know he points at Vengeance; we are cold,

And

And bafe ungrateful Wretches, if we fhun it:
Are we to hope for more Rewards or Greatnefs,
Or any thing but Death, now he is Dead?
Dar ft thou refolve? *Are.* I am perfect. *Phi.* Then like Flowers
That grew together all we'll fall together,
And with us that that bore us: When 'tis done,
The World fhall ftile us two deferving Servants:
I fear he will be before us. *Are.* This Night, *Phidias.*
  Phi No more.
  Max. Now worthy Friends I have done my mournings,
Let's burn this noble Body: Sweets as many
As Sun-burnt *Meroe* breeds, I'll make a Flame of
Shall reach his Soul in Heav'n: He that fhall live
Ten Ages hence, but to rehearfe this Story,
Shall with the fad Difcourfe on't darken Heav'n,
And force the painful Burdens from the Wombs
Conceiv'd a-new with Sorrow: Even the Grave
Where mighty *Sylla* fleeps fhall rend afunder
And give her fhadow up, to come and groan
About our Piles, which will be more, and greater
Than green *Olympus*, *Ida*, or old *Latmus*
Can feed with Cedar, or the Eaft with Gums,
Greece with her Wines, or *Theffaly* with Flowers,
Or willing Heav'n can weep for in her Showers.   [*Exe.*

ACT V. SCENE I.

Enter Phidias *with his Dagger in him, and* Aretus *poifon'd.*
Are. HE has his laft.
  Phi. Then come the worft of Danger,
Ætus, to thy Soul we give a *Cæfar;*
How long is't fince ye gave it him? *Are.* An hour,
Mine own two Hours before him: How it boils me!
  Phi It was not to be cur'd, I hope. *Are.* No, *Phidias,*
I dealt above his Antidotes: Phyficians
May find the Caufe, but where the Cure? *Phi.* Done bravely,
We are got before his Tyranny, *Aretus.*
  Are We had loft our worthieft end elfe, *Phidias.*
  Phi Canft thou hold out a while? *Are.* To torture him
Anger would give me leave, to live an Age yet;
That Man is poorly fpirited, whofe Life
Runs in his Blood alone, and not in's Wifhes.
And yet I fwell, and burn like flaming *Ætna,*
A thoufand new found Fires are kindled in me,
But yet I muft not dye this four Hours, *Phidias.*

Phi Remember who dyes with thee, and defpife Death.
Are. I need no Exhortation; the Joy in me,
Of what I have done, and why, makes Poifon Pleafure,
And my moft killing Torments, Miftreffes.
For how can he have time to die, or pleafure,
That falls as Fools unfatisfied, and fimple?
Phi. This that confumes my Life, yet keeps it in me,
Nor do I feel the danger of a dying,
And if I but endure to hear the Curfes
Of this fell Tyrant dead, I have half my Heav'n.
Are. Hold thy Soul faft but for four Hours, *Phidias*,
And thou fhalt fee to Wifhes beyond ours,
Nay more, beyond our Meanings.
Phi. Thou haft fteel'd me :
Farewel *Aretus*, and the Souls of good Men,
That as ours do, have left their *Roman* Bodies
In brave Revenge for Virtue, guide our Shadows.
I would not faint yet.   *Are.* Farewel, *Phidias*,
And as we have done nobly, Gods look on us.   [*Exe. feverally.*

SCENE II.

Enter Lycias, *and* Proculus.

Lyc. Sicker and ficker, *Proculus?*   *Pro.* Oh *Lycias*,
What fhall become of us? Would we had dy'd
With happy *Chilax*, or with *Balbus* Bed-rid,
And made too lame for Juftice.

Enter Licinius.

Licin The foft Mufick;
And let one fing to faften Sleep upon him ·
Oh Friends, the Emperor!   *Pro.* What fay the Doctors ?
Licin For us a moft fad faying, he is poifon'd,
Beyond all Cure too.   *Lyc.* Who?   *Licin.* The Wretch *Aretus*,
That moft unhappy Villain.   *Lyc.* How do you know it?
Licin. He gave him drink laft: Let's difperfe and find him;
And fince he has open'd Mifery to all,
Let it begin with him firft: Softly, he flumbers.

Enter Emperor fick in a Chair, with Eudoxia, *the Emprefs*, Phyficians,
and Attendants.

Mufick *and* Song.

Care-charming Sleep, thou Eafer of all Woes,
Brother to Death, fweetly thy Life difpofe
On this afflicted Prince, fall like a Cloud
In gentle Showers, give nothing that is loud;
Or painful to his Slumbers; eafie, fweet,
And as a purling Stream, thou Son of Night,

Pafs

Pass by his troubled-Senses ; sing his Pain
Like hallow murmuring Wind, or si ver Rain :
Into this Prince gently, oh gently slide,
And kiss him into Slumbers like a Bride.

Emp. Oh! Gods, Gods: Drink, Drink, colder, colder
Than Snow on *Scythian* Mountains: O my Heart strings!
Eud. How do's your Grace ?   *Phyf.* The Empress speaks, Sir.
Emp. Dying, dying, *Eudoxia*, dying.   *Phyf.* Good Sir, Patience.
Eud. What have ye given him ?   *Phyf.* Precious Things, dear Lady,
We hope shall Comfort him.   *Emp.* O flatter'd Fool,
See what thy God-head's come to : Oh *Eudoxia* !
            Enter Proculus, Licinius *with* Aretus.
Eud. O Patience, Patience, Sir.   *Emp. Danubius*
I'll have brought through my Body.   *Eud.* Gods give Comfort.
    Emp. And *Volga*, on whose Face the North Wind freezes.
I find an hundred Hells, an hundred Piles
Already to my Funerals are flaming,
Shall I not drink ?   *Phyf.* You must not, Sir.   *Emp.* By Heav'n
I'll let my Breath out that shall burn ye all
If ye deny me longer ; Tempests blow me,
And Inundations that have drank up Kingdoms
Flow over me, and quench me : Where's the Villain?
Am I immortal now, ye Slaves ? by *Numa*
If he do 'scape: Oh! oh !   *Eud.* Dear Sir.   *Emp.* Like *Nero*,
But far more terrible, and full of Slaughter,
I'th' midst of all my Flames I'll fire the Empire:
A thousand Fans, a thousand Fans to cool me:
Invite the gentle Winds, *Eudoxia*.   *Eud.* Sir.
    Emp. Oh do not flatter me, I am but Flesh,
A Man, a mortal Man: Drink, drink, ye Dunces ;
What can your Doses now do, and your Scrapings,
Your Oils, and Mithridates ? If I do die,
You only Words of Health, and Names of Sickness,
Finding no true Disease in Man but Mony,
That talk your selves into Revenues, oh!
And e'er you kill your Patients, beggar 'em,
I'll have ye flead, and dry'd.   *Pro.* The Villain, Sir;
The most accursed Wretch.   *Emp.* Be gone, my Queen,
This is no sight for thee   Go to the Vestals,
Cast holy Incense in the Fire, and offer
One powerful Sacrifice to free thy *Cæsar*.
    Pro. Go, go, and be Happy.   [*Exit* Eudoxia.
    Are. Go, but give no Ease,
The Gods have set thy last Hour, *Valentinian*,
Thou art but Man, a bad Man too, a Beast,
And like a sensual bloody Thing thou dyest.

                                        Pro.

Pro. Oh——Traitor !   *Are.* Curfe your felves ye Flatterers,
And howl your Miferies to come, ye Wretches,
You taught him to be poifon'd.   *Emp.* Yet no Comfort ?
    Are. Be not abus'd with Priefts, nor Pothecaries,
They cannot help thee: Thou haft now to live
A fhort half Hour, no more, and I ten Minutes:
I gave thee Poifon for *Æcius's* fake,
Such a deftroying Poifon would kill Nature;
And for thou fhalt not die alone, I took it.
If Mankind had been in thee at this Murder,
No more to People Earth again, the Wings
Of old Time clipt for ever, Reafon loft,
In what I had attempted; yet, O *Cæfar,*
To purchafe fair Revenge, I had poifoned them too.
    Emp. Oh Villain: I grow hotter, hotter.   *Are.* Yes;
But not near my Heat yet; what thou feel'ft now,
Mark me with horror *Cæfar,* are but Embers
Of Luft and Lechery thou haft committed.
But there be Flames of Murder.   *Emp.* Fetch out Tortures.
    Are. Do, and I'll flatter thee, nay more, I'll love thee:
Thy Tortures to what now I fuffer, *Cæfar,*
At which thou muft arrive too, e'er thou dy'ft,
Are lighter, and more full of Mirth than Laughter.
    Emp. Let 'em alone: I muft drink.   *Are.* Now be mad;
But not near me yet.   *Emp.* Hold me, hold me, hold me,
Hold me; or I fhall burft elfe.   *Are.* See me *Cæfar,*
And fee to what thou muft come for thy Murder;
Millions of Womens Labours, all Difeafes.
    Emp. Oh my afflicted Soul too!   *Are.* Womens Fears, Horrors,
Defpairs, and all the Plagues the hot Sun breeds——
    Emp *Æcius,* O *Æcius!* O *Lucina!*
    Are. Are but my Torments Shadows.
    Emp. Hide me Mountains;
The Gods have found my Sins: Now break.
    Are. Not yet, Sir;
Thou haft a pull beyond all thefe.   *Emp.* Oh Hell!
Oh Villain, curfed Villain!   *Are.* O brave Villain,
My Poifon dances in me at this deed:
Now *Cæfar,* now behold me, this is Torment,
And this is thine before thou dyeft, I am Wildfire:
The brazen Bull of *Phalaris* was feign'd,
The miferies of Souls defpifing Heav'n,
But Emblems of my Torments.
    Emp. Oh! Quench me, quench me, quench me,
    Are. Fire a Flattery;
And all the Poet's Tales of fad *Avernus,*

                                              To

To my Pains lefs than Fictions: Yet to fhew thee
What conftant love I boie my murder'd Mafter;
Like a South-wind, I have fung through all thefe Tempefts
My Heart, my wither'd Heart, fear, fear thou Monfter,
Fear the juft Gods, I have my Peace———   [*He dies.*

  Emp. More Drink,
A thoufand *April* Showers fall in my Bofom:
How dare ye let me be tormented thus?
Away with that prodigious Body, Gods,
Gods, let me afk ye what I am, ye lay
All your inflictions on me, hear me, hear me;
I do confefs I am a Ravifher,
A Murderer, a hated *Cæfar*; oh!
Are there not Vows enough, and flaming Altars,
The Fat of all the World for Sacrifice,
And where that fails, the Blood of thoufand Captives,
To purge thofe Sins? But I muft make the Incenfe:
I do defpife ye all, ye have no Mercy,
And wanting that, ye are no Gods, your Parole
Is only preach'd Abroad to make Fools fearful,
And Women made of Awe, believe your Heav'n:
Oh Torments, Torments, Torments, Pains above Pains,
If ye be any thing but Dreams, and Ghofts,
And truly hold the Guidance of Things mortal;
Have in your felves times paft, to come, and prefent,
Fafhion the Souls of Men, and make Flefh for 'em,
Weighing our Fates, and Fortunes beyond Reafon,
Be more than all the Gods, great in Forgivenefs;
Break not the goodly Frame ye build in Anger;
For you are things, Men teach u,, without Paffions,
Give me an Hour to know ye in: Oh fave me
But fo much perfect time ye make a Soul in,
Take this Deftruction from me; no ye cannot,
The more I would believe ye, more I fuffer,
My Biains are Afhes, now my Heart, my Eyes, Friends,
I go, I go, more Air, more Air; I am mortal.   [*He dies.*

  Pro. Take in the Body: Oh *Licinius*,
The Mifery that we are left to fuffer;
No pity fhall find us.   *Licin.* Our Lives deferve none:
Would I were chain'd again to flavery,
With any hope of Life.   *Pro.* A quiet Grave,
Or a Confumption now, *Licinius*,
That we might be too poor to kill, were fomething.
  Licin Let's make our beft ufe, we have Mony, *Proculus*,
And if that cannot fave us, we have Swords,
  Pro. Yes, but we dare not dye.   *Licin.* I had forgot, that:
                                 There's

There's other Countries then.   *Pro.* But the fame hate ftill,
Of what we are.   *Licin* Think any thing, I'll follow.

Enter a Meffenger.

Pro How now, what News?

Meff. Shift for your felves, ye are loft elfe:
The Soldier is in Arms for great *Æcius,*
And their Leutenant-General that ftop'd 'em,
Cut in a thoufand pieces : They march hither :
Befide, the Women of the Town have murder'd
Phorba, and loofe *Ardelia, Cæfar's* She-Bawds.

Licin. Then here's no ftaying, *Proculus. Pro.* O *Cæfar,*
That we had never known thy Lufts : Let's fly,
And where we find no Woman's Man let's dye.   [*Exe.*

SCENE III.

Enter Maximus.

Max. Gods, what a Sluce of Blood have I let open!
My happy Ends are come to birth, he's dead,
And I reveng'd ; the Empire's all a-fire,
And Defolation every where inhabits :
And fhall I live that am the Author of it,
To know *Rome* from the Awe o'th' World, the Pity ?
My Friends are gone before too, of my fending,
And fhall I ftay ? Is ought elfe to be liv'd for ?
Is there another Friend, another Wife,
Or any third holds half their Worthinefs,
To linger here alive for ? Is not Virtue
In their two everlafting Souls departed,
And in their Bodies firft Flame fled to Heav'n ?
Can any Man difcover this, and love me ?
For though my Juftice were as white as Truth,
My Way was crooked to it, that condemns me :
And now *Æcius,* and my honour'd Lady,
That were Preparers to my reft and quiet,
The Lines to lead me to *Elizium ;*
You that but ftept before me, on affurance
I would not leave your Friendfhip unrewarded,
Firft fmile upon the Sacrifice I have fent ye,
Then fee me coming boldly. Stay, I am foolifh,
Somewhat too fudden to mine own Deftruction,
This great end of my Vengeance may grow greater :
Why may not I be *Cæfar* ? Yet no dying ;
Why fhould I not catch at it ? Fools and Children
Have had that Strength before me, and obtain'd it,
And as the Danger ftands, my Reafon bids me,
I wil', I dare ; my dear Friends pardon me,
I am not fit to die yet, if not *Cæfar ;*

I

I am fure the Soldier loves me, and the People,
And I will forward, and as goodly Cedars
Rent from *Oeta* by a fweeping Tempeft
Jointed again, and made tall Mafts, defie
Thofe angry Winds that fplit 'em, fo will I
New-piece again, above the Fate of Women,
And made more perfect far, than growing private,
Stand and defie bad Fortunes : If I rife,
My Wife was ravifh'd well , If then I fall,
My great Attempt honours my Funeral.   [*Exit.*

SCENE IV.

Enter three Senators and Affranius.

1 *Sen.* Guard all the Pofterns to the Camp, *Afframus,*
And fee 'em faft, we fhall be rifled elfe ;
Thou art an honeft, and a worthy Captain.

2 *Sen* Promife the Soldier any thing   3 *Sen.* Speak gently,
And tell 'em we are now in Council for 'em.
Labouring to chufe a *Cæfar* fit for them,
A Soldier, and a Giver,   1 *Sen.* Tell 'em further,
Their free and liberal Voices fhall go with us

2 *Sen* Nay more, a Negative fay we allow 'em.

3 *Sen.* And if our Choice difpleafe 'em, they fhall name him.

1 *Sen.* Promife three Donatives, and large, *Affranius.*

2 *Sen.* And *Cæfar* once elected, prefent Foes,
With diftribution of all Neceffaries,
Corn, Wine and Oil.   3 *Sen.* New Garments, and new Arms,
And equal Portions of the Provinces
To them, and to their Families for ever.

1 *Sen.* And fee the City ftrengthned.

Affra. I fhall do it.   [*Exit* Affranius.

2 *Sen. Sempronius,* thefe are woful Times.   3 *Sen.* O *Brutus* !
We want thy Honefty again ; thefe *Cæfars,*
What noble Confults got with Blood, in Blood
Confume again, and fcatter.   1 *Sen.* Which way fhall we?

2 *Sen* Not any way of Safety I can think on.

3 *Sen* Now go our Wives to Ruin, and our Daughters,
And we Beholders, *Fulvius.*   1 *Sen.* Every thing
Is every Man's that will.   2 *Sen.* The Veftals now
Muft only feed the Soldier's Fire of Luft,
And fenfual Gods be glutted with thofe Offerings,
Age like the hidden Bowels of the Earth
Open'd with Swords for Treafure.   Gods defend us,
We are Chaff before their Fury elfe.   2 *Sen* Away,
Let's to the Temples.   1 *Sen* To the Capitol,
'Tis not a time to Pray now, let's be ftrengthen'd.

Exit.

Enter Affranius.

3 Sen. How now *Affranius:* What good News? *Affra.* A Cæfar.

1 Sen. Oh! Who? *Affra.* Lord *Maximus* is with the Soldier,
And all the Camp rings *Cæfar, Cæfar, Cæfar;*
He forc'd the Emprefs with him for more Honour.

2 Sen. A happy Choice: Let's meet him. *3 Sen* Bleffed Fortune.

1 Sen. Away, away, make room there, room there, room.

[*Exeunt Senators. Flourish.*

Within. Lord *Maximus* is *Cæfar, Cæfar, Cæfar;*
Hail *Cæfar Maximus.* *Affra.* Oh turning People!
Oh People excellent in War, and govern'd;
In Peace more raging than the furious North,
When he ploughs up the Sea, and makes him Br ne,
Or the loud falls of *Nile;* I muft give way,
Although I neither love nor hope this.
Or like a rotten Bridge that dares a Current,
When he is fwell'd and high crackt, and Farewel.

Enter Maximus, Eudoxia, *Senators and Soldiers.*

Sen Room for the Emperor *Sold.* Long Life to *Cæfar.*

Affra. Hail *Cæfar Maximus.* *Emp. Max.* Your Hand, *Affranius.*
Lead to the Palace, there my Thanks in general,
I'll fhower among ye all: Gods give me Life,
Firft to defend the Empire, then you Farhers,
And valiant Friends, the Heirs of Strength and Virtue,
The Rampiers of old *Rome,* of us the Refuge;
To you I open this Day all I hive,
Even all the hazard that my Youth hath purchas'd,
Ye are my Children, Family, and Friends,
And ever fo refpected fhall be, forward.
There's a Profcription, grave *Sempronius,*
'Gainft all the Flatterers, and lazy Bawds
Led loofe-liv'd *Valentinian* to his Vices,
See it effected. [*Flourish.*

Sen Honour wait on *Cæfar.*

Sold. Make room for *Cæfar,* there. [*Exe. all but* Affra.

Affra Thou haft my Fears,
But *Valentinian* keeps my Vows: Oh Gods!
Why do we like to feed the greedy Raven
Of thefe blown Men, that muft before they ftand,
And fixt in Eminence, caft Life on Life,
And trench their Safeties in with Wounds, and Bodies?
Well 'ro ard *Rome,* thou wilt grow weak with changing,
And die without an Heir, that lov'ft to breed
Sons f r the killing hate of Sons: For me,
I only live to find an Enemy. [*Exit.*

S C E N E

SCENE V.

Enter Paulus, *a Poet;* and Licippus, *a Gentleman.*

Pau. When is the Inauguration? *Licip.* Why, to Morrow.

Pau. 'Twill be short time. *Licip.* Any device that's handsome.
A *Cupid,* or the God o'th' Place will do it,
Where he must take the Fasces. *Pau.* Or a Grace.

Licip. A good Grace has no Fellow. *Pau.* Let me see,
Will not his Name yield something? *Maximus*
By th' way of Anagram? I have found out *Axis,*
You know he bears the Empire. *Licip.* Get him Wheels too,
'Till be a cruel Carriage else. *Pau.* Some Songs too.

Licip. By any means some Songs: But very short ones,
And honest Language *Paulus,* without bursting,
The Air will fall the sweeter. *Pau.* A Grace must do it.

Licip. Why, let a Grace then. *Pau.* Yes, it must be so;
And in a Robe of blue too, as I take it.

Licip. This Poet is a little Kin to th' Painter
That could paint nothing but a ramping Lion,
So all his learned Fancies are blue Graces.

Pau. What think ye of a Sea-nymph, and a Heav'n?

Licip. Why what should she do there, Man? There's no Water.

Pau. By th' Mass, that's true, it must be a Grace, and yet
Methinks a Rain-bow. *Licip.* And in Blue. *Pan.* Oh yes!
Hanging in Arch above him, and i'th' middle.

Licip. A shower of Rain. *Pau.* No, no, it must be a Grace.

Licip. Why prithee Grace him then. *Pau.* Or *Orpheus,*
Coming from Hell. *Licip.* In Blue too. *Pau.* 'Tis the better,
And as he rises, full of Fires *Licip.* Now Bless us,
Will not that spoil his Lute-strings, *Paulus?* *Pau.* Singing,
And crossing of his Arms. *Licip.* How can he play then?

Pau. It shall be a Grace, I'll do it. *Licip.* Prithee do,
And with as good a Grace as thou canst possible;
Good Fury *Paulus,* be i'th' Morning with me,
And pray take Measure of his Mouth that speaks it. [*Exe.*

SCENE VI.

Enter Maximus *and* Eudoxia.

Max. Come my best lov'd *Eudoxia:* Let the Soldier
Want neither Wine, nor any thing he calls for,
And when the Senate's ready give us Notice;
In the mean time leave us,
Oh my dear Sweet! *Eud.* Is't possible your Grace
Should undertake such Dangers for my Beauty,
If it were Excellent? *Max* By Heav'n 'tis all
The World has left to brag of. *Eud.* Can a Face

I 2   Long

Long since bequeath'd to Wrinkles with my Sorrows,
Long since raz'd out o' th' Book of Youth and Pleasure,
Have power to make the strongest Man o'th' Empire,
Nay the most stay'd, and knowing what is Woman,
The greatest aim of Perfectness Men liv'd by,
The most true, constant lover of his Wedlock,
Such a still blowing Beauty Earth was proud of,
Lose such a noble Wife, and wilfully;
Himself prepare the way, nay make the Rape?
Did ye not tell me so?   *Max.* 'Tis true *Eudoxia.*

   Eud. Lay desolate his dearest piece of Friendship,
Break his strong Helm he steer'd by, sink that Virtue,
That Valour, that even all the Gods can give us,
Without whom he was nothing, with whom worthiest,
Nay more, arrive at *Cæsar,* and kill him too,
And for my sake? Either ye love too dearly,
Or deeply ye dissemble, Sir.   *Max.* I do so;
And 'till I am more-strengthen'd, so I must do;
Yet would my Joy, and Wine had fashion'd out
Some safer Lie.—— Can these things be, *Eudoxia,*
And I dissemble? Can there be but Goodness
And only thine, dear Lady, any end,
Any Imagination but a left one,
Why I should run this Hazard? O thou Virtue!
Were it to do again, and *Valentinian,*
Once more to hold thee, sinful *Valentinian,*
In whom thou wert set, as Pearls are in salt Oysters,
As Roses are in rank Weeds, I would find
Yet to thy sacred self a dearer Danger,
The Gods knows how I honour thee.   *Eud.* What love, Sir,
Can I return for this, but my Obedience?
My Life, if so you please, and 'tis too little.

   Max. 'Tis too much to redeem the World.
   Eud. From this Hour,
The Sorrows for my dead Lord, fare ye well,
My living Lord has dry'd ye; and in Token,
As Emperor this Day I honour ye,
And the great Caster new of all my Wishes,
The Wreath of living Lawrel, that must compass
That sacred Head, *Eudoxia* makes for *Cæsar:*
I am methinks too much in love with Fortune;
But with you, ever Royal Sir, my Maker,
The once more Summer of me, meer in Love,
Is poor Expression of my Doting.   *Max.* Sweetest.

   Eud. Now of my Troth ye have bought me dear, Sir.
   Max. No, had I at loss of Mankind.

                               Enter

Enter a Meffenger.

Eud. Now ye flatter.

Meff. The Senate waits your Grace.   *Max.* Let 'em come on,
And in a full Form bring the Ceremony:
This Day I am your Servant, Dear, and proudly
I'll wear your honour'd Favour.   *Eud.* May it prove fo.   [*Exeunt.*

SCENE VII.

Enter Paulus *and* Licippus.

Licip Is your Grace done?   *Pau.* 'Tis done.

Licip. Who fpeaks?   *Pau.* A Boy

Licip. A dainty blue Boy, *Paulus?*   *Pau* Yes.

Licip Have ye view'd the Work above?

Pau Yes, and all up, and ready

Licip The fm rts does you fimple Honour, *Paulus,*
The Wreath your blue Grace muft prefent, fhe made.
But hark ye, for the Soldiers?   *Pau* That's done too:
I'll bring 'em in, I warrant ye.   *Licip.* A Grace too?

Pau. The fame Grace ferves for both.   *Licip.* About it then
I muft to the Cup-board; and be fure, good *Paulus,*
Your Grace be fiting, that he may hang cleanly:
If there fhould need another Voice, what then?

Pau I'll hang another Grace in.   *Licip* Grace be with ye. [*Exeunt.*

SCENE VIII.

Enter in State Maximue, Eudoxia, *with Soldiers and Gentlemen of*
Rome, *the Senators, and R ds a d xes born before them*
  A ynnet with }   { With a Banquet prepar'd with
  Trumpets   }   { Hautboys, Mufick, Sing. Wreath

3 Sen Hail to thy Imperial Honour facred *Cæfar,*
And from the old *Rome* take thefe Wifhes;
You holy Gods, that hitherto have held,
As Juftice holds her Ballance equal pois'd,
This glory of our Nation, this full *Roman,*
And made him fit for what he is, confirm him:
Look on this fon, O *Jupiter,* our helper,
And *Romulus,* thou Father of our Honour,
Preferve him like thy felf, Juft, Valiant, Noble,
A Lover and Increafer of his People;
Let him begin with *Numa,* ftand with *Cato,*
The firft five Years of *Nero* be his Wifhes,
Give him the Age and Fortune of *Emylius,*
And his whole Reign, renew a great *Auguftus.*

SONG.

Honour that is ever living,
Honour that is ever giving,

Honour

Honour that sees all and knows,
Both the Ebbs of Man and Flows;
Honour that rewards the best,
Sends thee thy rich Labour's rest;
Thou hast studied still to please her,
Therefore now she calls thee Cæsar;
Chorus. *Hail, hail,* Cæsar, *hail and stand,*
And thy Name out-live the Land,
Noble Fathers, to his Brows,
Bind this Wreath with thousand Vows.

All. Stand to Eternity.   *Max.* I thank ye, Fathers,
And as I rule, may it still grow or wither·
Now to the Banquet, ye are all my Guests,
This Day be liberal Friends, to Wine we give it;
And smiling Pleasures: Sir, my Queen of Beauty;
Fathers, your Places: These are fair Wars, Soldiers,
And thus I give the first charge to ye all;
You are my Second, Sweet, to every Cup,
I add unto the Senate, a new Honour,
And to the Sons of *Mars* a Donative.

S O N G.

God Lycus *ever young,*
Ever Honour'd, ever Sung;
Stain'd with Blood of lusty Grapes,
In a thousand lusty Shapes;
Dance upon the Mazers brim,
In the Crimson Liquor swim;
From thy plenteous Hand Divine,
Let a River run with Wine;
God of Youth, let this day here
Enter neither Care nor Fear.

Boy. Bellona's Seed, the Glory of old *Rome,*
Envy of conquer'd Nations, nobly come,
And to the fulness of your warlike noise
Let your Feet move, make up this hour of Joys;
Come, come I say, range your fair Troop at large,
And your high measure turn into a Charge.
Semp. The Emperor's grown heavy with his Wine.
Affr. The Senate stays, Sir, for your thanks.   *Semp.* Great *Cæsar.*
Eud. I have my wish.   *Affr.* Wilt please your Grace speak to him.
Eud. Yes, but he will not hear, Lords.
Semp. Stir him, *Lucius;* the Senate must have thanks.
2 Sen. Luc. Your Grace, Sir, *Cæsar.*
Eud. Did I not tell you he was well: He's dead.

Semp.

Semp. Dead? Treason, guard the Court, let no Man pass;
Soldiers, your *Cæsar's* murder'd. *Eud* Make no tumult,
Nor arm the Court, ye have his Killer with ye;
And the just cause, if ye can stay the hearing:
I was his Death; that Wreath that made him *Cæsar*,
Has made him Earth. *Sold.* Cut her in thousand pieces.

Eud Wise Men would know the Reason first: To die,
Is that I wish for, *Romans,* and your Swords,
The heaviest way of Death: Yet Soldiers grant me,
That was your Empress once, and honour'd by ye,
But so much time to tell ye why I kill'd him,
And weigh my Reasons well, if Man be in you;
Then if ye dare, do cruelly condemn me.

Affr Hear her ye noble *Romans,* 'tis a Woman,
A Subject not for Sword, but Pity: Heav'n,
If she be guilty of malicious Murder,
Has given us Laws to make Example of her;
If only of Revenge, and Blood hid from us,
Let us consider first, then execute.

Semp. Speak, bloody Woman. *Eud.* Yes. This *Maximus,*
That was your *Cæsar* Lords, and noble Soldiers,
(And if I wrong the dead, Heav'n perish me;
Or speak to win your Favours, but the Truth)
Was to his Country, to his Friends, and *Cæsar,*
A most malicious Traitor. *Semp* Take heed, Woman.

Eud. I speak not for Compassion. Brave *Æcius,*
(Whose blessed Soul, if I lye, shall afflict me,)
The Man that all the World lov'd, you ador'd,
That was the Master-piece of Arms, and Bounty;
Mine own Grief shall come last: This Friend of his,
This Soldier, this your right Arm, noble *Romans,*
By a base Letter to the Emperor,
Stufft full of Fears, and poor Suggestions,
And by himself unto himself directed,
Was cut off basely, basely, cruelly;
Oh Loss, oh Innocent! Can ye now kill me?
And the poor Stale, my noble Lord, that knew not
More of this Villain, than his forced fears,
Like one foreseen to satisfie, dy'd for it:
There was a Murder too, *Rome* would have blush'd at;
Was this worth being *Cæsar?* or my Patience? nay, his Wife,
By Heav'n he told it me in Wine, and Joy,
And swore it deeply, he himself prepar'd
To be abus'd, how? let me grieve, not tell ye,
And ween the Sins that did it: And his end
Was only me, and *Cæsar:* But me he ly'd in.

These

These are my Reasons, *Romans,* and my Soul
Tells me sufficient; and my Deed is Justice:
Now as I have done well, or ill, look on me.

  Affr. What less could Nature do, what less had we done,
Had we known this before? *Romans,* she is righteous;
And such a piece of Justice Heav'n must smile on.
Bend all your Swords on me, if this displease ye,
For I must kneel, and on this virtuous hand
Seal my new Joy and Thanks, thou hast done truly.

  Semp Up with your Arms, ye strike a Saint else, *Romans.*
May'st thou live ever spoken our Protector:
Rome yet has many noble Heirs Let's in
And pray before we chuse, then plant a *Cæsar*
Above the reach of Envy, Blood, and Murder.

  Affr Take up the Body, nobly to his Urn,
And may our Sins and his together burn.

                       [*Exeunt. A dead March.*

EPILOGUE.

WE wou'd fain please ye, and as fain be pleas'd;
  'Tis but a little liking both are eas'd:
We have your Mony, and you have our Ware,
And to our Understanding good and fair
For your own Wisdom's sake be not so mad,
T' acknowledge ye have bought things dear and bad
Let not a brack i'th' Stuff or here and there
The fading Gloss a general Loss appear:
We know ye take up worse Commodities,
And dearer pay. yet think your Bargain's wise;
We know in Meat and Wine, ye fling away
More Time and Wealth, which is but dearer Pay,
And with the Reckoning all the Pleasure lost.
We bid ye not unto repenting Cost.
The Price is easie, and so light the Play,
That ye may new digest it every Day
Then noble Friends, as ye would chuse a Mistress,
Only to please the Eye a while, and kiss,
'Till a good Wife be got: So let this Play
Hold ye a while, until a better may.

FINIS.

CPSIA information can be obtained at www.ICGtesting.com
Printed in the USA
BVOW09s2215101215

429975BV00011B/116/P